Models-based Practice in Physical Education

This book offers a comprehensive synthesis of over 40 years of research on models in physical education to suggest Models-based Practice (MbP) as an innovative future approach to physical education. It lays out the ideal conditions for MbP to flourish by situating pedagogical models at the core of physical education programs and allowing space for local agency and the co-construction of practice.

Starting from the premise that true MbP does not yet exist, the book makes a case for the term "pedagogical model" over alternatives such as curriculum model and instructional model, and explains how learners' cognitive, social, affective and psychomotor needs should be organised in ways that are distinctive and unique to each model. It examines the core principles underpinning the pedagogical models that make up MbP, including pedagogical models as organising centres for program design and as design specifications for developing local programs. The book also explores how a common structure can be applied to analyse pedagogical models at macro, meso and micro levels of discourse. Having created a language through which to talk about pedagogical models and MbP, the book concludes by identifying the conditions – some existing and some aspirational – under which MbP can prosper in reforming physical education.

An essential read for academics, doctoral and post-graduate students, and pre-service and in-service teachers, *Models-based Practice in Physical Education* is a vital point of reference for anyone who is interested in pedagogical models and wants to embrace this potential future of physical education.

Ashley Casey is Senior Lecturer in Pedagogy at Loughborough University, UK and Series Editor of the *Routledge Focus on Sport Pedagogy*.

David Kirk is Professor of Education at the University of Strathclyde, UK, Honorary Professor of Human Movement Studies at the University of Queensland, Australia and Series Editor of the *Routledge Studies in Physical Education and Youth Sport*.

Routledge Studies in Physical Education and Youth Sport

Series Editor: David Kirk

University of Strathclyde, UK

The *Routledge Studies in Physical Education and Youth Sport* series is a forum for the discussion of the latest and most important ideas and issues in physical education, sport, and active leisure for young people across school, club and recreational settings. The series presents the work of the best well-established and emerging scholars from around the world, offering a truly international perspective on policy and practice. It aims to enhance our understanding of key challenges, to inform academic debate, and to have a high impact on both policy and practice, and is thus an essential resource for all serious students of physical education and youth sport.

Also available in this series

www.routledge.com/Routledge-Studies-in-Physical-Education-and-Youth-Sport/book-series/RSPEYS

Models-based Practice in Physical Education

Ashley Casey and David Kirk

Routledge
Taylor & Francis Group

LONDON AND NEW YORK

First published 2021
by Routledge
2 Park Square, Milton Park, Abingdon, Oxon OX14 4RN

and by Routledge
52 Vanderbilt Avenue, New York, NY 10017

Routledge is an imprint of the Taylor & Francis Group, an informa business

British Library Cataloguing-in-Publication Data
A catalogue record for this book is available from the British Library

Library of Congress Cataloging-in-Publication Data
A catalog record for this book has been requested

ISBN: 978-0-367-33332-4 (hbk)
ISBN: 978-0-429-31925-9 (ebk)

Typeset in Times New Roman
by Apex CoVantage, LLC

Ash and David: To all the pupils, teachers and researchers who experienced, adopted, researched and refined pedagogical models. You envisioned and enacted a new future for physical education, and we are grateful to you all for that.

Ash: I normally dedicate my books to Sarah, Thomas and Maddie, but not this time.
To Maddie, Thomas and Sarah
Because Maddie is tired of being named last just because she's the youngest.
And to Mum, who hopes one day I'll learn to spell words (tautology) but knows I probably won't.

Contents

Figures

Tables

Preface

The lineage of this book can be traced back to the summer of 2003. It was the first time that we worked together. David was the teacher and Ash was the student (in the traditional sense at least) on a masters' degree module at Loughborough University entitled "School Based Evaluation." Ash's assignment "Leadership, Cooperation and Responsibility Through Sport Education" became a foundation stone of his work in what we now term Models-based Practice. As did his rationale for the study: "I want to change **me**, the way **I** teach, and the way my pupils learn."

We would argue that that is a tenuous link to this book, but every oak needs an acorn. We have grown that acorn for nearly two decades – both collectively but more often separately. We have studied and problematised and written and problematised and presented and problematised, and here we are still writing and problematising MbP. We agreed on much and disagreed on some, and this book has seen a narrowing of that gap. We are on the same page. Literally in this case. But we still have a few small bones of contestation. Models as verbs not nouns for example. Still, we are united in our belief that MbP is a potential future for physical education. We are on the same page when it comes to pedagogical models and their worth to physical education. We are both anti multi-activity, sport technique-based teaching and pro the multi-model curriculum. Therefore, we invite you to step into this book with an open mind and with questions and concerns. We do so in the hope that we can, collectively, do better for the generations of young people who come under our care.

We were completing the writing of this book when the Covid-19 pandemic swept over us, with a complete lockdown in the UK where we live occurring late in March 2020. It may surprise some readers, given the extent to which the pandemic has dominated our daily lives over the past (and entirely unprecedented) three months, that we make no mention of the virus and the ways it seems to have utterly changed the world. We have resisted writing the consequences of the pandemic for education systems into our thinking about MbP in physical education not because we don't acknowledge their profundity, but because we believe what we are advocating for MbP as an alternative approach to physical education is entirely consistent with these consequences. We need now more than ever forms of physical education that are fair, inclusive and equitable. This is important since the pandemic has revealed just how prevalent precarity, inequality and injustice are in so many societies around the world. It is also important for school systems that are paid for through taxes on citizens. This recurrent annual investment of public money must show benefits, educationally and in terms of health and well-being, for all children. We hope this book can make a small contribution to addressing these needs.

Ash and David,
June 2020

1 Why models-based practice?

A positive approach

A typical approach to answering the question "Why models-based practice?", and thus making a case for an alternative to the dominant form of physical education, is to point out the shortcomings of the dominant form. Enright, Hill, Sandford, and Gard (2014) have argued that to do so is to engage in "deficit scholarship," which, they suggest, is prevalent in physical education, particularly among socially critical researchers. Supporting this concern, McMillan (2017) argues that talking down physical education teachers is both unfair and inaccurate since there is a tendency in socially critical research to mischaracterise and overlook good teaching. We agree with both authors to the extent that only to highlight shortcomings, deficiencies and failures for the sake of critique is inappropriate. At the same time, we think it is important to face the "brutal facts" of our situation if we are to comprehend where we are and why (Cohen, 2007). Identifying shortcomings is also a means of judging the extent to which the alternative we proposed offers a better educational experience for all students than that which they currently "enjoy."

Our starting point, therefore, is to take a positive approach and point out why we can't afford *not* to have high quality physical education in primary and secondary schools. In doing this we echo Cathy Ennis (2014) who noted that the health of school students was the first of seven Cardinal Principles of the American National Education Association in 1918. She wrote:

> Many citizens still believe that we should fund physical education *after* we fund everything else. In fact, the opposite is the case. We need to reverse this perception! Student-centered learning in sport and physical activity serves as the foundation for a lifetime of healthy decision-making. It is what all of us and especially the most vulnerable people in our society depend on for future well-being. It must come *first*.
>
> (Ennis, 2014, p. 68)

As Kirk (2020) has recently pointed out, while health has been a recurring preoccupation among physical educators for over 100 years, conceptions of health within physical education have shifted since 1918, from a medico-health and posture-focused rationale to the currently popular notion that exercise is medicine (Sallis, 2009). From this latter perspective, school physical education is viewed as a means of managing the risks, inherent in sedentary lifestyles, of cardio-vascular disease and obesity. Influenced by the New Public Health, Sallis and McKenzie (1991) proposed that physical educators join with other health-related professionals to form intra-professional teams to combat these diseases. Nearly 20 years later, McKenzie, this time with Lounsbery (McKenzie & Lounsbery, 2009) makes the case for Moderate to Vigorous Physical Activity (MVPA) as a key feature of lessons in schools, though they bemoan the fact (and staying with the medicine analogy) that all too often physical education is "the pill not taken."

Fitzpatrick (2018) more recently argued that to take health as a starting point in a rationale for alternative forms of physical education, as Oliver and Kirk (2015) do in their work with adolescent girls, is to buy into this risk-management agenda, with its "questionable" capacity to genuinely benefit women's lives while reproducing gendered inequalities. While Fitzpatrick's point is well made, we don't think that this connection between health and a risk-management approach is a given. We think Ennis's mention of "vulnerable people" takes us in another direction from the pathogenic concerns of physical education as a form of "medicine" to a salutogenic position which lies at the heart of McCuaig, Quennerstedt, and Macdonald's (2013) advocacy for a "strength-based" approach. Building on the work of Antonovsky (1979), a psychologist of stress who asked "What are the *salutary* factors that keep people healthy?", Quennerstedt (2008), McCuaig et al. (2013), and McCuaig and Quennerstedt (2018) have applied a salutogenic theory of health promotion to curriculum development in physical education. These authors adopted a key feature of Antonovsky's approach and asked, "How do people stay healthy?" rather than "how do we reduce the risk of people becoming sick?"

Antonovsky (1979) argued that the common denominator in empirical studies of healthy people was that their lives had a Sense of Coherence, insofar as they were meaningful, comprehensible and manageable. Healthy people are able to access what he calls Generalised Resistance Resources (GRRs), specific to their circumstances, that individuals and communities can draw on to keep them healthy. By way of example, Ferreira's (2019) empirical research has shown how physical activity programs are one source of GRRs that support a Sense of Coherence among older people.

McCuaig and Quennerstedt (2018), among others, argue that school physical education can provide access to GRRs that contribute to a Sense of Coherence. But in order to do so, it needs to take particular forms. As we will see shortly when we come to discuss the shortcomings of the currently dominant form of physical education, this positive and educationally beneficial effect is unlikely. Staying for now with the question of why we can't afford *not* to have quality physical education in schools, we can note that for the rising numbers of young people living in or at risk of living in precarity, access to GRRs is limited (Kirk, 2020). State funded school physical education, free at the point of delivery, is for many of these young people the *only* access they may have to engage in physical activity programs and to develop the physical competences and knowledge for human wellbeing. This is not just an individual good but, as Ennis points out, benefits society as a whole.

> Personal health is the asset on which our economies, our sustenance, our livelihoods, and our ways of life depend. Today, we need to secure our futures by investing in our physical capital through high quality physical education programs that establish strong foundations of health and well-being. This investment is essential and timely, not an afterthought.
>
> (Ennis, 2014, p. 11)

In many countries the importance of physical education is recognised, particularly where it is a required part of the curriculum in both primary and secondary schools, where specialist facilities and equipment are available, and where teachers have specific qualifications in the field. In such places the bill to the public purse, funded through taxation, can be considerable. Even for a small country such as Scotland, for example, with a population of approximately 5.5 million and just under 700,000 children and young people attending state schools, the cost represents a serious government commitment. Kirk (2020) estimated that, in Scotland, the cost of physical education teachers' salaries alone is around £80 million per year. The majority of these teachers are in secondary schools, arguably a misplaced resource in itself (Kirk, 2005). This figure does not take into account facilities, equipment, teacher education programs in universities, nor funding for school inspection. We suggest this outlay is likely to be similar in other countries, proportionate to their size, where physical education is a required subject in schools. Taxpayers would reasonably expect to see tangible benefits to children and young people for recurrent spending on this scale. And indeed, we want to argue that physical education funded in this way *can* provide genuine and evident educational benefits for all children. But not in its current form.

We begin to make a case for Models-based Practice (MbP), then, from a positive perspective. We believe children and young people, particularly those who are socially vulnerable and growing up in precarity, cannot afford *not* to experience high quality physical education. This is because some of the GRRs that assist children and young people to stay healthy can be sourced in the physical competencies, knowledge, motivation and values developed in and through physical education. Our view is that inclusive, fair and equitable forms of physical education, free at the point of delivery in state schools can, along with other quality educational experiences, contribute to young people's sense of the meaningfulness, comprehensibility and manageability of their lives. This is only possible, we think, if physical education in its currently dominant form is changed. In order for change to happen, we need to face the brutal facts about this dominant but failing approach.

Multi-activity, sport technique-based physical education

The currently dominant form of physical education in schools, possibly more so in secondary than primary (Griggs, 2015), is multi-activity, and is practised in sport technique-based programs (Kirk, 2010). These programs first appeared in schools in Britain in the post-World War Two era, during the 1950s and 1960s, and in other places a little earlier (e.g. the USA, Ennis, 2014) or a little later (e.g. in Brazil, Costa & Tubino, 2005). Pühse and Gerber's (2005) edited collection of accounts of physical education in 35 countries suggests that the multi-activity, sport technique-based approach is a global phenomenon, notwithstanding important local variations on this theme (Larsson & Quennerstedt, 2016). Indeed, this form of physical education seems able to persist regardless of the existence of diverse national curricula in many countries. The shortcomings of this approach are documented and widely accepted by physical education scholars (Ennis, 2014; Kirk, 2010; Locke, 1992), if not the teaching profession more broadly (McMillan, 2017), and don't need to be rehearsed in detail again here. It is nevertheless worth highlighting, for the purpose of answering the question "why MbP?", three issues with the multi-activity, sport technique-based approach.

The first issue is that this dominant approach to physical education is not inclusive of all young people. There is a strong body of research, produced over many years, that shows the children and young people who benefit most from multi-activity, sport technique-based physical education are "just like" their teachers (Ennis, 2014), who as Standal (2015) describes them, are White, relatively affluent, and "severely able-bodied." Multi-activity, sport technique-based physical education, according to this research, underserves many children and young people who are from ethnic minority backgrounds, who live in precarity, who are disabled, and who are female. Moreover, many children and young people are underserved by the dominant form of physical education because they belong to more than one of these groups, further compounding their adverse experiences. This well-documented *exclusion* of a significant proportion of the school population from the educational benefits of physical education is unacceptable, given the amounts of public funding spent on its provision year on year.

We need to stress here that we do not believe this situation is in any way an intentional outcome of the work teachers do under very challenging circumstances. Nor do we believe that this situation is an intentional outcome of policymakers who are often seeking to produce inclusive curricula in the face of growing diversity among school-age children and young people. Indeed, much of the research literature is critical of the failure of the physical education community, as a whole, to be as responsive as we should be to constant changes in the circumstances of children and young people. The rising prevalence of precarity in Britain, and its mal-effects on the health and wellbeing of vulnerable people after more than a decade of austerity, is just one example of an emerging crisis that seems to be passing physical educators by (Kirk, 2020). In contrast, we believe positive action for appropriate change to school physical education is essential in response to such examples of significant social change.

A second issue is to understand *how* multi-activity, sport technique-based physical education excludes a significant proportion of children and young people from benefitting educationally. It excludes some children and young people because multi-activity, sport technique-based physical education does not recognise nor cater for the diversity among the school-age population, neither in terms of physical endowment, nor embodied subjectivities. It is, according to its critics, hypernormative and heteronormative, a form of "straight pedagogy" that seeks to "correct" the queerness of bodies (McGlashan & Fitzpatrick, 2017; Landi, 2018; Standal, 2015). This process of "straightening queerness" is not only concerned with gender and sexuality. It is, in crude terms, a matter of overlooking the exceptionality all young people bring to physical education classes. It does this in favour of a collective, narrowly defined and stereotypical norm of appropriate body shape, physical competence, and the "right" attitude.

Again, we stress that this is not something teachers intend to do, at least not most teachers for the most part. Straight pedagogy is borne out of necessity in terms of the ways in which schools as institutions are organised, the purposes they serve in society, and their unavoidable hidden curricula. The "industrial-age school" continues to be the dominant institutional form of the school, operating within and informed by late 19th and 20th century forms of industrial capitalism, even when many countries of the Global North are primarily neoliberal, post-industrial capitalist societies. Through its primary instruments of the timetable and the classroom, the industrial age school seeks to construct young people who "fit" and who are "fit for" particular adult roles in society. Lawson (2008) explains how this institutional form of the school works in the case of the USA:

> The industrial age American school has been oriented toward workforce preparation for the factory and the assembly line, and the school's social organization has followed suit. . . . Justified as a meritocratic system, schools and their constituent subjects have served as sorting machines . . ., and too often these schools reproduced the existing class structure. . . . To facilitate student sorting, both curricula and instruction have been organized in part to find out which students had aptitude for particular subjects. Like products moving along an assembly line, students have been required to move from one class to another to receive the same standardized treatment (the same instruction and the same teaching methods-as-training), complete performance exams, receive a grade indicative of aptitude, ability, and also to determine their work discipline, persistence, and effort. . . . PE has been just another stop on the assembly line, subject to the same industrial logic, rules, ideology, and regulations as other subjects. Especially in sport-dominated programs, young people are sorted and labelled, developing identities as athletes and non-athlete.
>
> (Lawson, 2008, pp. 10–11)

While Lawson provides a powerful critique of school and its socially and educationally inequitable effects, we should not read this as inevitable. The industrial age school does not *determine* children's and young people's futures. For instance, the notion of school as a meritocracy has been used on both sides of the political divide to argue that schools, through this sifting and sorting function, either promote or deny equality of opportunity (Ball, 2017). Bourdieu's notion of cultural capital is often deployed in such arguments as a means of explaining class-based inequalities in educational attainment, though there is a lack of consistent empirical evidence for this straightforward association (Tzanakis, 2011). Nevertheless, schools located within societies that have embraced a free-market model of education, such as England (Ball, 2017), exacerbate these processes of sifting and sorting children and young people to fit roles in life to which they are allegedly suited, thereby greatly reducing social mobility (Social Mobility Commission, 2019). A multi-activity, sport technique-based form of physical education is ideally suited to this purpose of sifting and sorting according to aptitude and ability, each of which is defined by the straight pedagogy of these dominant physical education programs. The industrial age schools' institutional form and purposes inform this dominant form of physical education. It thus works to rank children and young people explicitly. It is by definition an exclusionary, inequitable and normative form of school practice. A challenge for any alternative proposal for physical education is to take account of and counter the exclusionary, unfair and inequitable nature of this institutional form of education.

A third issue relates to the internal organisation of this dominant form of physical education. Multi-activity programs consist of relatively short units of lessons, sometimes as few as four to six lessons on one physical activity, before a switch is made to a new activity. As such, the multi-activity curriculum rarely offers students opportunities to develop physical competences and knowledge about and through physical activity in any depth. Such brief exposure to a fixed array of physical activities (which are often revisited year after year (Siedentop, 2002)) arguably impedes individual learning progression. Moreover, in classes of 30 or more students, with wide ranging motivation for and competence in specific activities, even the most capable teacher is likely to be challenged to provide worthwhile educational experiences for all children and young people. Like Ennis (1999), we acknowledge that highly competent, motivated and energetic teachers have, mainly through their strength and dedication, used multi-activity physical education effectively for many years. But these teachers are the exception and not the rule. Conversely, and using the words of Ennis (1999, p. 32), we argue that:

> to the untrained observer it appears that students [in a multi-activity approach to physical education] are involved and participating in a variety of sport and exercise opportunities. A closer look, however, reveals several curricular structures that promote inequality and (re) produce gender segregation and low-skill levels in both boys and girls.

Even in highly supportive education systems, where lessons are scheduled for up to 50 minutes two to three times per week, there is little possibility that learners can ever move beyond basic competencies. Importantly, and regardless of the nature of the physical activity, the wide range of sports and games that make up this form of physical education must be shoehorned into short units of lessons that individually occupy 50 minutes of timetabled time.

It is little wonder, therefore, that teachers tend to focus on sport techniques, rather than the sports themselves, in order to optimise what benefits they can for their students. Further difficulty arises from the nature of the facilities made available for physical education in schools. In many affluent countries these spaces comprise playing fields, sports halls, fitness suites and, occasionally, swimming pools. These "classrooms" tell us much about the assumptions architects and their advisors make about the nature of physical education, just as "60ft x 30ft gymnasia, fully equipped" (in the words of Dave Munrow (1963)) defined the form of "physical education as-gymnastics" (Kirk, 2010, p. 88). As a consequence of these challenging circumstances, for which programs based on multi-activity, sport technique-based physical education were invented, Daryl Siedentop (2002, p. 372) once famously remarked that the "same introductory lesson gets taught again, and again, and again."

These three issues with multi-activity, sport technique-based physical education illustrate that critique of this ubiquitous form of practice is not merely a matter of finding deficits. If we have a commitment as a community of practice of physical educators to forms of physical education that are inclusive, fair and equitable, then it is necessary that we confront the brutal facts of the currently dominant form of physical education. Indeed, as Ennis (1999, p. 32) suggested "no curriculum in physical education has been as effective in constraining opportunities and alienating girls [and as Casey & Larsson, 2018, p. 443 added "non-sporty boys"] as that found in co-educational, multi-activity sport classes."

We have argued thus far that multi-activity, sport technique-based physical education is neither inclusive, fair, nor equitable, no matter how hard teachers try to make it work. This is because of its hyper- and heteronormativity, its reflection of the industrial age schools' sifting and sorting purpose, and its internal structure. The shortcomings of multi-activity, sport technique-based physical education cannot, then, be attributed to any one group. By confronting the brutal facts of where we are now and why, we are not in the business of finger-pointing and blaming. On the contrary, we believe in facing the reality of our current situation before we attempt to advocate for an alternative. Given the considerable amount of public funds assigned to run physical education programs in many countries, there is much at stake.

Advocating models-based practice

In advocating for MbP as an alternative to replace multi-activity, sport technique-based physical education, we think there are at least four principles underpinning pedagogical models that need to be outlined prior to considering the substance of this alternative in detail.

1 A new organising centre for program design: the "pedagogical model"

The pedagogical model is a foundational element in MbP. We prefer the term pedagogical to either curriculum or instructional models used in other approaches to MbP, which we discuss in Chapter 2. This is because the word pedagogical better captures the constitutive elements of the model (i.e. curriculum, teaching, learning, and assessment). At the same time, we acknowledge Metzler's (2000) important contribution through his proposal that use of the term "model" shifts the focus from methods of teaching individual classes to larger scale program design. In multi-activity, sport technique-based physical education, content is the main organising principle. A good example of the application of this is the 2007 National Curriculum Physical Education for England, with its main organisers of games, gymnastics, aquatics, athletics, outdoor activities and dance.

For pedagogical models, the main constitutive elements are curriculum, teaching, learning and assessment. These four elements are interactive and interdependent, and together offer the definition of pedagogy that we will work with in this book. The main organising principle for a MbP approach to physical education, then, is these four interactive and interdependent elements taken together. Another way to think about this is that these four elements together become the "unit of analysis" for designing physical education programs in schools.

It becomes immediately apparent that this shift in the organising centre of physical education programs creates possibilities that are often not evident nor obvious in multi-activity, sport technique-based physical education. For example, a pedagogical model thus defined allows the identification of learning aspirations and the alignment of curriculum, teaching and assessment for their most effective realisation. This alignment of the four elements of pedagogy addresses a serious shortcoming of multi-activity program designs where it is common to find a range of learning aspirations – for example, skill development, motivation, tactical decision-making and physical fitness – all being pursued through the same activity. It also addresses the commonplace use of only a few teaching styles, typically directive, task-based and reciprocal, regardless of the subject matter or the learning aspirations. Moreover, the shift in organising centre from content to pedagogical model makes explicit the importance of assessment in physical education, something which has caused physical educators serious and chronic challenges (Hay & Penney, 2012). In multi-activity programs, and with a proliferation of learning aspirations, teachers often resort to tick-box checklists to reduce the complexity of the task of assessment or look for particular methods of instruction that worked in the past. When specific learning aspirations are stated and curriculum and teaching aligned to real-ise them, assessment becomes more clearly relevant and manageable.

2 The "curriculum-as-specification": sustainable adaptation

A second principle underpinning a MbP approach to physical education is the idea, derived from the work of Lawrence Stenhouse (1975), that the "curriculum," or in this case the pedagogical models that make up school physical education, should be regarded as a specification for practice, rather than a prescribed list of content or teaching and learning experiences. As a specification for practice, a pedagogical model is always to be viewed as provisional, in the sense that regular and ongoing adaptation of plans and programs will be necessary at local level to meet new contingencies and sets of circumstances. For example, a new cohort of children in a class brings new capabilities and interests, new personalities and new classroom dynam-ics. If physical education is to be inclusive, fair and equitable, it is unlikely that last year's program will be suitable for this year's cohort, at least not in its entirety.

The notion of curriculum-as-specification also rested on Stenhouse's most well-known contribution to the educational research literature of "teacher-as-researcher." Curriculum is a specification for practice rather than a prescription, because teachers will experiment with, and try out, dif-ferent teaching and learning strategies and assessment practices over the course of a physical education program. What worked with one class may not work with another. While the notion of teacher-as-researcher sounds very formal, it was intended first and foremost to capture the nature of teachers' work as a process of learning from their own and others' practices. It is in this sense that curriculum-as-specification is a form of sustainable adaptation. In this context, then, we will consider pedagogical models to be design specifications, not prescriptions, for the development of local physi-cal education programs.

3 The eternal tension: balancing local agency
and external support

Curriculum-as-specification illustrates the principle that pedagogical models are design specifications for program development rather than programs in themselves. This is a crucially important distinction since it is intended to manage the eternal tension in educational policy and practice between agency at a local level and external support, advice and prescription. The word "manage" is used deliberately. We are not claiming that the pedagogical model as design specification resolves this tension.

The notion does, however, rest on a belief that agency at local level is not merely desirable but essential to high quality physical education in practice. Teachers are key players. They are experts in the local context of implementation (Kirk & Macdonald, 2001). They are better placed than anyone external to the school to know their students, the physical and cultural environment, including traditions, and the local stakeholders, particularly parents and community organisations. Their experience on the ground is unique and invaluable to identifying the needs and interests of their students. That said, without the confidence or willingness to move beyond the control exerted by printed schema in every school or district – schema that dictate what can and cannot be taught and when students are ready for this knowledge – then local agency loses its potential to enact change.

Moreover, teachers cannot carry out their multi-faceted work by themselves. Ennis (2014, p. 9) provides the cautionary example of the USA, where the education system is highly decentralised, and for subjects like physical education, "there is little oversight or interest." In many other countries of the Global North, as we already noted, national curricula provide "broad and bold" (Organization for Economic Cooperation and Development, 2015) designs that on the one hand specify children's and young people's entitlements by law to a free education and what that consists of, and on the other guidance to schools in local jurisdictions about how these entitlements might be realised. Ideally, there is space in these guidelines for schools and teachers to make decisions that reflect local needs and interests. Pedagogical models as design specifications are intended to work within national curricula, where these exist, to provide more specific support to schools and teachers than guidelines can reasonably achieve.

4 Co-construction of physical education: teachers, students, stakeholders

A fourth principle closely related to the notion of the need for local agency is that school physical education programs based on pedagogical models will not be constructed by teachers alone. They will also include students and other stakeholders at specific points in the program planning and implementation process. This notion of curriculum co-construction is common in some pedagogical models such as activist approaches to working with adolescent girls (Oliver & Kirk, 2016) and with socially vulnerable youth (Luguetti, Oliver, Kirk, & Dantas, 2017). This notion not only reflects democratic ideals that educational programs are done *with* rather than *to* young people, but also advocates student-centred educational practice.

Conclusion

Central to this chapter has been the need to face the brutal fact that the dominant, multi activity, sport technique-based approach to physical education is not capable of supporting or enhancing the lives of all young people (Ennis, 2014). Consequently, and globally, the public pay many millions (in whichever currency you choose) to provide the teachers, buildings and resources for teaching physical education through a fundamentally flawed approach. As Larry Locke (1992) once pointed out, this is no-one's fault, but is the stark reality that prompts us to write this book.

In answering the question "Why models-based practice?", and thus making a case for MbP as an alternative to the dominant form of physical education, we outlined four principles that inform the pedagogical models that constitute MbP, which are: (1) a new organising centre for program design; (2) pedagogical models are specifications for practice in schools; (3) they permit us to manage the tension between local agency and external support; and (4) they require co-construction of physical education by teachers, students, stakeholders. Common to these four principles is the understanding that curriculum, teaching, learning and assessment, which make up pedagogy, become a foundational unit of analysis for designing physical education programs in schools. Crucially, we argued that a handful of directive task-based reciprocal teaching styles are being used regardless of subject matter or learning aspiration. In place of such styles we proposed pedagogical models as design specifications for practice, and curriculum as something that is provisional rather than preordained (as seen in both national curriculum documents and local schemes of work). Finally, we reasoned that when pedagogical models are viewed as design specifications for program development, rather than programs themselves, teachers and other stakeholders are key players. Fundamentally, however, to move to a MbP approach – especially when faced with externally devised and orchestrated schema – requires the willingness and confidence to allow students, teachers and others to practice with physical education.

In the next chapter, we turn to address the notion of MbP itself, and how this concept is differently understood within the scholarly and practice communities.

References

Antonovsky, A. (1979). *Health, stress, and coping*. San Francisco: Jossey-Bass.

Ball, S. J. (2017). *The education debate* (3rd ed.). Bristol: Policy Press.

Casey, A., & Larsson, H. (2018). "It's groundhog day": Foucault's governmentality and crisis discourses in physical education. *Quest, 70*(4), 438–455.

Cohen, R. (2007). *The second bounce of the ball: Turning risk into opportunity*. London: Weidenfield & Nicholson.

Costa, V., & Tubino, M. (2005). Brazil. In U. Puhse & M. Gerber (Eds.), *International comparison of physical education concepts, problems, prospects* (pp. 132–149). Aachen: Meyer & Meyer.

Ennis, C. D. (1999). Creating a culturally relevant curriculum for disengaged girls. *Sport, Education and Society, 4*(1), 31–49.

Ennis, C. D. (2014). What goes around comes around . . . or does it? Disrupting the cycle of traditional, sport-based physical education. *Kinesiology Review, 3*, 63–70.

Enright, E., Hill, J., Sandford, R., & Gard, M. (2014). Looking beyond what's broken: Towards an appreciative research agenda for physical education and sport pedagogy. *Sport, Education and Society, 19*(7), 912–926.

Ferreira, H. J. (2019). *Health and physical education professionals' salutogenic and pedagogical practices for working with disadvantaged older adults* (Unpublished PhD thesis). Sao Paulo State University, Rio Claro.

Fitzpatrick, K. (2018). Poetry in motion: In search of the poetic in health and physical education. *Sport, Education and Society, 23*(2), 123–134.

Griggs, G. (2015). *Understanding primary physical education*. London: Routledge.

Hay, P., & Penney, D. (2012). *Assessment in physical education: A sociocultural perspective*. London: Routledge.

Kirk, D. (2005). Physical education, youth sport and lifelong participation: The importance of early learning experiences. *European Physical Education Review, 11*(3), 239–255.

Kirk, D. (2010). *Physical education futures*. London: Routledge.

Kirk, D. (2020). *Precarity, critical pedagogy and physical education*. London: Routledge.

Kirk, D., & Macdonald, D. (2001). Teacher voice and ownership of curriculum change. *Journal of Curriculum Studies, 33*(5), 551–567.

Landi, D. (2018). Toward a queer inclusive physical education. *Physical Education and Sport Pedagogy, 23*(1), 1–15.

Larsson, H., & Quennerstedt, M. (2016). Same, same but different: (Re)understanding the place of context in physical education practice. *Recherches & Educations, 15*, 69–86.

Lawson, H. A. (2008). *Crossing borders and changing boundaries to develop innovations that improve outcomes*. The Cagigal Lecture, AIESEP World Congress, Sapporo.

Locke, L. F. (1992). Changing secondary school physical education. *Quest, 44*(3), 361–372.

Luguetti, C., Oliver, K. L., Kirk, D., & Dantas, L. (2017). Exploring an activist approach of working with boys from socially vulnerable backgrounds in a sport context. *Sport, Education and Society, 22*(4), 493–510.

McCuaig, L., & Quennerstedt, M. (2018). Health by stealth – exploring the sociocultural dimensions of salutogenesis for sport, health and physical education research. *Sport, Education and Society, 23*(2), 111–122.

McCuaig, L., Quennerstedt, M., & Macdonald, D. (2013). A salutogenic, strengths-based approach as a theory to guide HPE curriculum change. *Asia-Pacific Journal of Health, Sport and Physical Education, 4*(2), 109–125.

McGlashan, H., & Fitzpatrick, K. (2017). LGBTQ youth activism and school: Challenging sexuality and gender norms. *Health Education, 117*(5), 485–497.

McKenzie, T. L., & Lounsbery, M. A. F. (2009). School physical education: The pill not taken. *American Journal of Lifestyle Medicine, 3*, 219–225.

McMillan, P. (2017). Understanding physical education teachers' day-to-day practice: Challenging the "unfair" picture. In M. Thorburn (Ed.), *Transformative learning and teaching in physical education* (pp. 159–175). London: Routledge.

Metzler, M. W. (2000). *Instructional models for physical education*. Scottsdale, AZ: Holcomb Hathaway.

Munrow, A. D. (1963). *Pure and applied gymnastics* (2nd ed.). London: Bell.

Oliver, K. L., & Kirk, D. (2015). *Girls, gender and physical education: An activist approach*. New York: Routledge.

Oliver, K. L., & Kirk, D. (2016). Towards an activist approach to research and advocacy for girls and physical education. *Physical Education and Sport Pedagogy, 21*(3), 313–327.

Organization for Economic Cooperation and Development (OECD). (2015). *Improving schools in Scotland: An OECD perspective*. Paris: OECD.

Pühse, U., & Gerber, M. (Eds.). (2005). *International comparison of physical education: Concepts, problems, prospects*. Aachen: Meyer & Meyer.

Quennerstedt, M. (2008). Exploring the relation between physical activity and health – a salutogenic approach to physical education. *Sport, Education and Society, 13*(3), 267–283.

Sallis, J. F. (2009). Measuring physical activity environments: A brief history. *American Journal of Preventive Medicine, 36*, S86–S92.

Sallis, J. F., & McKenzie, T. L. (1991). Physical education's role in public health. *Research Quarterly for Exercise and Sport, 62*(2), 124–137.

Siedentop, D. (2002). Content knowledge for physical education. *Journal of Teaching in Physical Education, 21*, 368–377.

Social Mobility Commission. (2019). *State of the nation 2018–19: Social mobility in Great Britain*. London: HMSO.

Standal, O. F. (2015). *Phenomenology and pedagogy in physical education.* London: Routledge.

Stenhouse, L. (1975). *An introduction to curriculum research and development.* London: Heinemann.

Tzanakis, M. (2011). Bourdieu's social reproduction thesis and the role of cultural capital in educational attainment: A critical review of key empirical studies. *Educate, 11*(1), 76–90.

2 What is models-based practice?

Introduction

Even a casual reader of the literature on "models" in physical education will have encountered a range of terminology and numerous interpretations of key terms. Despite this appearance of divergence, we think there is a lot of commonality among scholars' and practitioners' intentions when working with the notion of "models." We see this commonality as positive and productive. It is important, at the same time, to make clear our own position on the use of the notion of "models" in physical education and, in particular, what we mean by the central concept of this book: Models-based Practice (MbP). We need to explain why we are writing "based" in lower case. We also need to explain why we prefer the term pedagogical model as the basic unit of MbP rather than other commonly used terms such as curriculum model (Lund & Tannehill, 2014), instructional model (Gurvitch, Lund, & Metzler, 2008) and teaching model (Cothran & Kulinna, 2008).

Models-based practice in physical education

There are varying degrees of precision in the ways scholars in physical education refer to "Models-Based Practice" (MBP). Some authors use the term relatively indiscriminately to refer to any situation in which a "model" of some kind (pedagogical, curriculum, instructional) is used (e.g. Dudley, Goodyear, & Baxter, 2016). The plural "models" is still used in these situations, even if authors are only referring to the use of a single model. Some use the term MBP somewhat indiscriminately to describe a range of innovative approaches to physical education such as Sport, Physical Activity and Recreation for Kids (SPARK) and Dynamic Physical Education (Dyson, Kulinna, & Metzler, 2016). This occurs even when, arguably, such approaches may not be widely recognised as "models." Metzler (2000) uses the term *Model-Based Instruction* (MBI) in his work on instructional models, which, as we will explain later, we think is consistent with some key aspects of our use of MbP here.

Put simply, we believe that rather than using the acronym MBP indiscriminately to represent both the use of a single model and multiple models in a curriculum, "Models-based" (lower case b) should be viewed as an adjective that describes practice in physical education. So, what might MbP look like, and why are we interested in a phenomenon that does not as yet exist? Two key ideas assist us to answer these questions: (1) the organising centre, and (2) a multi-model approach.

The first idea is that within MbP the pedagogical model becomes what Metzler (2017) calls the "organising centre" for program planning and development. Typically, in multi-activity, sport technique-based physical education, content is the organising centre, such as games, aquatics, dance and so on. We interpret Metzler's notion of an organising centre to include content, but also teaching, learning and assessment taken together as an irreducible unit. We also borrow from Metzler's organising centre notion that a model will take into account various features of the context in which it will be practised, the resources available in that context and the characteristics of teachers and students.

The second idea is that MbP does not refer to the use of one model, but many (i.e. two or more). For us, the term MbP only applies when we are considering a multi-model approach to physical education. Casey (2014) credits Siedentop and Tannehill (2000) and Metzler (2000) with the first mention of this idea, but it is clear that this was also the intention of Jewett and Bain (1985) in the first edition of *The Curriculum Process in Physical Education*. In a diagram on page 17 of that first edition of their book, which was later to be omitted from the 1995 second edition (see Jewett, Bain, & Ennis, 1995), Jewett and Bain clearly convey their notion of a multi-model approach to physical education, resulting moreover in a wide variety of "local curricula," a point we will come to later in this chapter.

Despite the variance in terminology within the literature, these two ideas feature (albeit less overtly) in most advocacies for models-based approaches, including Jewett et al. (1995), Metzler (2000), Siedentop and Tannehill (2000) and Lund and Tannehill (2014). Use of the term "model" implies that content is not the sole organiser for program planning and development. Moreover, few, if any, advocates for models-based approaches appear to propose that there is one best way to practice physical education, even if they use the notion of MBP indiscriminately to apply to a single model.

MbP then has at least these two signal features. But as we have just proposed, so do all other major advocacies for models-based approaches.

We will have more to say about MbP in a moment and its additional characteristics, with the lower case b distinguishing this particular version from others more often characterised as MBP or MBI.

First, though, what of Casey's (2014, p. 30) claim that "true MBP does not yet exist in our literature"? We think, at a literal level, this claim is not quite accurate in the sense that there are no examples at all of approaches to physical education where these two signal features apply. Casey is a case in point. Over the last decade he has reported using several models when he worked as a secondary school teacher (e.g. Casey & Dyson, 2009; Casey & MacPhail, 2018). Gurvitch et al. (2008) have also written about their use of MBI in the Physical Education Teacher Education (PETE) program at Georgia State University. We are also aware of other institutions, including our own, where attempts have been made to take a models-based approach to PETE, though these are not necessarily in the public domain. Lund and Tannehill (2014) provide one of the very few published examples of a models-based approach to physical education program planning and development at school district level, with a consistent approach from K-12.

This latter example is important because it comes very close to our own preferred concept of MbP, where multiple models become the organising centres for individual teachers, in and across school programs and, as guidance at least, at school, district, regional and national levels. This qualification is important, as we point out later in this chapter, when considering how MbP assists us in managing the tension between local agency and external support. It is in this sense, as an aspect of curriculum policy and routine practice, that Casey (2014) was correct to claim that "true MBP does not yet exist." We have many examples in the research literature of the implementation of single models, with varying degrees of success, in schools, universities and community settings. Mostly, in the case of schools, this has involved parachuting the pedagogical model into a multi-activity, sport technique-based form of physical education, with resultant challenges for timetabling, facilities and teacher professional learning, as some of our recent research has illustrated (Kirk et al., 2018). What we lack, with the exceptions just noted, is a research literature on "true MbP" in physical education.

In this sense, i.e. that "true MbP does not exist," ours and others' advocacies for models-based approaches to physical education are aspirational. We do not know empirically, beyond the very few examples cited, if such an approach can work to provide high quality physical education. Any proposal for MbP as we define this term is therefore "theoretical." We think there are all sorts of good reasons why it *should* work. Some of these reasons rest on empirical evidence of the critical mass of research on single model implementation and development. What we *can* say with confidence is that multi-activity, sport technique-based physical education is not fit for purpose, as we demonstrated in Chapter 1. We do not merely assume, however, that MbP is the right or only response to this failure. What we require (and which we hope this book provides) is a sound rationale for this approach, and an explanation of how we think it could work to benefit all school-aged young people, and under what conditions.

We have established thus far that MbP is informed by two key ideas, that pedagogical models are the organising centres for physical education program planning and development, and the need to take a multi-model approach. Moreover, and despite differences in terminology among the scholarly community, we think we have established that these two ideas are common to most advocacies for models-based approaches to physical education. Before we can elaborate more fully on the nature of MbP, however, and despite the touchstones these two ideas provide, we need to detail the differences in the terminology currently in use. We do this in order to judge the extent to which this divergence may simply be semantics, or ascertain whether it signals more substantial and significant differences of emphasis and purpose.

Divergences in key terminology: why we prefer pedagogical model

We have already stated here and elsewhere (e.g. Casey, 2014, 2016; Kirk, 2013) that our preference is for the term pedagogical model over the others most regularly in use i.e. curriculum and instructional models. We reiterate our arguments to date, which have been that the word pedagogy refers to the interdependent and interacting features of curriculum, teaching, learning and assessment, rather than the words curriculum and instruction which refer to aspects of the pedagogical process. We also note that pedagogy is always shaped by the context in which it is enacted. These four features of pedagogy form an irreducible unit. This means that although we may focus on and foreground one or another of these features for a given purpose, in practice all four are always present in school physical education settings, formally or informally.

The alignment of these features is of utmost importance, and is the feature of pedagogical models that is often lacking in traditional practice. In constructing a pedagogical model, we engage in what Lund and Tannehill (2014) call "backward design," identifying the aspirations we have for student learning, and align curriculum, teaching and assessment in ways that lead to the realisation (as far as this is possible) of these aspirations. We use the term aspirations rather than outcomes because we believe it is not possible to know precisely the affect a teacher may have on learners, particularly when working in the affective domain (Luguetti, Oliver, Dantas, & Kirk, 2017). Learning aspirations will relate specifically to the main idea or theme of the model. In multi-activity, sport technique-based physical education, in contrast, learning "outcomes" are often specified across several domains with little or no differentiation in learning tasks, teaching styles and assessment practices.

We recognise that this definition of pedagogy, although widely accepted in many parts of the Anglophone scholarly community, is not universal nor is it used consistently. For example, it is not uncommon to find scholars writing about "curriculum and pedagogy," particularly in the US, where "pedagogy" here (seems to) include teaching and learning. Nevertheless, it appears to us that when curriculum models and instructional models are discussed they tend to embrace the four features of what we call pedagogy, i.e. teaching, learning, curriculum and assessment. For example, Metzler writes:

> An effective instructional model will have a comprehensive and coherent plan for teaching that includes a theoretical foundation, statements of intended learning outcomes, teacher's needed content knowledge expertise, developmentally appropriate and sequenced learning activities, expectations for teacher and student behaviors, unique task structures, measures of learning outcomes, and mechanisms for assessing the faithful implementation of the model itself.
>
> (Metzler, 2017, p. 9)

Similarly, in a discussion of curriculum models, Lund and Tannehill (2014) emphasise the importance of what they call "instructional alignment" in terms of "1) what we intend for students to learn, 2) how we assess to determine their success, and 3) what and how we teach." Likewise, Jewett et al. (1995, p. 15, original emphasis) proposed that, "a *curriculum model* . . . incorporates identification of goals, selection and structuring of program content, and development of instructional procedures and learning environments."

In all these accounts of instructional and curriculum models we can see at least three of the four features of pedagogy are present, albeit expressed in specific ways. On the basis of this analysis, it would appear that we have merely semantic differences. In substance therefore, regardless of the actual descriptor of the model used, pedagogical, instructional and curriculum models effectively embrace the four features of curriculum, teaching, and assessment and their careful alignment to realise particular aspirations for learning. Beyond pointing out that use of the descriptors "instructional" and "curriculum" have the potential to misrepresent the nature of the models to a careless reader, and that the term "pedagogical" more accurately describes what kind of model we are talking about, we can be relaxed about the divergence in use of these terms. Conceptually, therefore, we are surely on the same page with our view of pedagogical models as those who advocate for curriculum and instructional models.

Before we agree or disagree, there are two further issues we need to address with regard to this divergence of model terminology: one that is indeed more substantive and another that has to do with the translatability of these Anglophone words into other languages.

The more substantive issue is the proposal that curriculum and instructional models refer to program planning and development at different levels of generality and specificity. For example, in their introduction to a 2016 special issue of the *Journal of Teaching in Physical Education* (JTPE) on "Models Based Practice in Physical Education," Dyson, Kulinna, and Metzler stated:

> MBP occurs on two levels – curriculum, and instruction. Curriculum level MBP starts with the intended student learning outcomes for a school or district's physical education program – over the span of an entire academic year, or perhaps from Pre/Kindergarten through grade 12. From those outcomes emerges (sic) what Lund and Tannehill (2014) have called Main Theme Curriculum models that are designed specifically to promote those preferred long-term learning outcomes. In effect, MBP at the curriculum level provides a program with its mission, primary content, identity, and infrastructure – all for the purpose of allowing more students to achieve its priority long-term learning outcomes. . . . MBP can also be used to define and guide teaching and learning within content units and individual lessons – instructional MBP. At this level, MBP promotes short-term learning outcomes, and is used by teachers to align key instructional practices like class management, learning activities, social learning, pedagogical decisions, and assessment with specific unit and lesson objectives.
>
> (Dyson et al., 2016, p. 297)

This distinction between curriculum and instructional models is certainly supported by the uses of these terms more broadly, away from specific concern with models. For example, in a discussion of the question "what is curriculum?", Jewett et al. (1995) claim scholars:

> Differ on the use of the term *curriculum* as it relates to *instruction*. Curriculum is frequently used as a broad, generic term, including instruction. When a distinction between the two is drawn, curriculum is defined as an educational agency's plan for facilitating learning; instruction is defined as the delivery system, or the aggregate of educative transactions, that constitutes the teaching-learning process for implementing the plan. The major focus is on ends, on the 'why' and 'what' questions; instruction tends to emphasize means, or the 'how' questions. While the two can be discussed separately for analytical purposes, in practice they are interactive and inseparable.
>
> (Jewett et al., 1995, p. 12)

Thus, the distinction Dyson et al. make between curriculum and instructional models seems to rest on a more widely accepted distinction between these two terms. Having made this distinction clearly, Dyson et al. somewhat confuse the matter by arguing that some models operate at both curricular and instructional levels. Adding to this confusion Metzler, himself, a leading advocate for the concept of instructional models, wrote:

> Instructional models are based on an alignment of learning theory, long-term learning goals, context, content, classroom management, related teaching strategies, verification of process, and the assessment of student learning. Joyce and Weil (1980) define an *instructional model* as 'a plan or pattern that can be used to shape curriculums (long-term courses of studies), to design instructional materials, and to guide instruction in the classroom and other settings' (p. 1). An instructional model should be used for an entire unit of instruction and includes all of the planning, design, implementation, and assessment functions for that unit.
>
> (Metzler, 2017, p. 8)

Metzler's account of instructional models seems to contradict both the distinction made by Dyson et al. and the more general account by Jewett and colleagues. The apparent difference between these accounts prompts us to ask whether it is useful to make such a distinction between different kinds of models, since the main axis of differentiation appears to be levels of generality and specificity (which we feel is an inevitably slippery task). We wonder, in particular, whether this level of nuance is likely to be helpful for widespread adoption of the notion of MbP by teachers. In any case, as we progress with our account of MbP, we think this distinction makes less sense when we consider how models might have been originally proposed (see Chapter 3), then used specifically, in schools and other sites of pedagogical practice (see Chapters 4 and 5). This distinction, in short, seems to introduce a layer of complexity into discussions of MbP that is unnecessary and possibly misleading and unhelpful.

A second and related concern is to do with language. Curriculum is an Anglophone term which has no precise equivalent in closely related languages such as Spanish and French where the English word "curriculum" tends to be used (e.g. Kirk, 1990). Equally instruction is not widely used outside the US, at least not in school physical education contexts, where teaching is mostly preferred. Importantly, there exists clear equivalent terms for teaching in most languages. Pedagogy is another term that has no precise equivalent in languages that share their origins with English. In French, the term *didactique* is arguably close in meaning to pedagogy, in the sense that it refers to inter-related aspects of physical educational practices such as teaching, learning and curriculum, though typically refracted through the prism of knowledge (Amade-Escot, 2000). There are similar words in Spanish (*didactica*) and German and Nordic countries (*didaktik*) with similar meanings (Hopmann, 2007). Of course, didactic often has a pejorative connotation in English usage which we think rules out an argument for didactical models.

Our point is that it is most unlikely to be useful to scholars from language communities other than English for there to be a proliferation of terms to describe the use of models in the planning and development of physical education programs, especially when some of these terms do not translate easily into their mother tongues. Having pointed this issue out, we remain convinced that the words pedagogy and pedagogical (in the ways we have defined these terms here) are probably the most useful since they may translate more easily into concepts already widely in use in language communities that share their historical roots with English. This said, we consider that this is one issue that may be best left to the physical education scholarship "marketplace." Having read about and listened to the arguments, individual researchers will make their own choices of preferred terminology.

The practice architectures of pedagogical models

We wrote in Chapter 1 that the pedagogical model is a foundational element in MbP. Having supplemented this idea with the notion that the model is the organising centre for physical education program planning and development, we need to say a little more about what we think pedagogical models "are" in terms, first of all, of their internal structure or "practice architectures" (Goodyear, Casey, & Kirk, 2017). We have already stated that pedagogical models rest on a definition of pedagogy as the interacting and interdependent elements of curriculum, teaching, learning and assessment. We have also noted that the use of any pedagogical model will always require some consideration of the context of that use. Finally, we emphasised the importance of the alignment of these key elements, in particular curriculum, teaching, and assessment, in order to facilitate the realisation of learning aspirations. It is in this sense, i.e. of an irreducible unit, that a model can be viewed as an organising centre for physical education program planning and development. In this planning and development process these four key interacting and interdependent elements will always be in play, as will consideration of their context of use.

The theory of practice architectures, originally derived from the work of Kemmis and Grootenboer (2008), suggests that every practice enacted in classrooms is a result of semantic (e.g. language), social (e.g. power relations) and physical (e.g. materials) spaces (Goodyear et al., 2017). Kemmis et al. (2014, p. 31, original emphasis) described their view of practice architectures as:

> (a) individual and collective practice shapes and is shaped by (b) what we will describe as *practice architectures*, so that (c) the *sayings*, *doings* and *relatings* characteristic of the practice hang together in *projects* that in turn shape and are shaped by (d) practice traditions that encapsulate the history of the happenings of the practice, allow it to be reproduced, and act as a kind of collective 'memory' of the practice. The practice architectures that enable and constrained practices exist in three dimensions parallel to the activities of *saying*, *doing* and *relating*. They constitute enabling and constraining preconditions of the conduct of practices.

Expanding on the notion of practice architectures, Kemmis et al. (2014) argued that they consist of three sets of arrangements. Cultural-Discursive arrangements are found in the domain of language (i.e. *sayings*) and enable and constrain what can be said when describing, explaining and justifying practice. Material-Economic arrangements occur in the physical space (*doings*) which, in turn, facilitate or limit what can be done in the gymnasiums and classrooms available to teachers. Social-political arrangements encompass power, solidarity and social space (*relatings*) and pertain to the functions, practices and rules of a given organisation. Whilst these *sayings*, *doings* and *relatings*, or cultural-discursive, material-economic and social-political arrangements, can all operate in isolation they became practice architectures as and when we ask the question "What are we doing?" Practice, in terms of practice architectures, is a complex and temporal undertaking that was recently defined by Kemmis as:

> a form of human action in history, in which particular activities (*doings*) are comprehensible in terms of particular ideas and talk (*sayings*), and when the people involved are distributed in particular kinds of relationships (*relatings*), and when the combination of sayings, doings and relatings 'hangs together' in the project of the practice (the ends and purposes that motivate practice).
>
> (Kemmis, 2018, pp. 2–3, emphasis added)

Building on this definition, Kemmis (2019) went on to argue that practice, thought of in this way, was scalable from the macro (in our case of models themselves), through the meso of our conduct with a model (i.e. single model MBP), to the micro ("moment-by-moment talk and interaction that unfolds in practices as they are performed" (p. 13)). In explaining the relationship between the different aspects of practice architectures, Kemmis et al. (2014, p. 34, original emphasis) wrote:

> a living practice becomes part of the *happening* that unfolds in a particular place, part of the happening *of* that practice, part of its existence and being in time. The practice takes up sayings, doings and relatings already to be found in the site, *orchestrates* and engages with them, and leave behind in the setting particular kinds of discursive, physical and social traces or residues of *what happened* through the unfolding of the practice. These traces and residues are left not only in participants' memories and interactional captivities but also in the practice itself as a site for sociality. Some of these residues become part of the practice architectures of the setting and newly encountered by others who subsequently inhabit it.

We think the concept of practice architectures has great potential for exploring and expressing the internal structures of pedagogical models. Drawing in the work of Schatzki (2002), Kemmis (2019) suggests that practice architectures prefigure practices without determining them. The use, therefore, of particular "technical" language or *sayings* (e.g. the main idea), the requirement for specific social relations or *relatings* (e.g. co-construction) and the designation of particular physical spaces for teaching and learning or *doings* (e.g. playing fields) *taken together* make particular pedagogical models possible.

Within this concept of practice architectures, and in addition to the definition of pedagogy we just noted, all pedagogical models contain two further preconfigured features: a main idea and critical elements.

The main idea, which is similar to Lund and Tannehill's (2014) notion of "main theme" curriculum models, seeks to capture and communicate the main purpose and character of a particular model. For example, advocating for the development of a pedagogical model for health-based physical education, Haerens, Kirk, Cardon, and De Bourdeaudhuij (2011) claimed that the main idea or theme was "pupils valuing the physically active life," a concept they borrowed from Siedentop (1996). Luguetti et al.'s (2017) pedagogical model for working with socially vulnerable youth identifies "co-constructing empowering possibilities through sport for youth from socially vulnerable backgrounds" as its main idea. For Williams and Wainwright's (2016) prototype pedagogical model for outdoor adventure education, the main idea is "personal growth through adventure." Authors vary in their choice of main idea, even when models take a similar approach. For example, Metzler (2017) selects for an instructional model for tactical games the main idea or theme as "teaching games for understanding." Advocating for a pedagogical model for teaching games in school physical education based on Bunker and Thorpe's (1982) teaching games for understanding, Kirk (2017) selected the main idea of "the production of thinking players." Whichever terminology is chosen, the words should convey what distinguishes one model from another in terms of its main characteristics and purposes.

Critical elements relate to and further develop Metzler's (2000) notion of teacher and student benchmarks. Critical elements provide a pedagogical model with its distinctive "shape" as well as giving users some sense of what the creators of the model regard as its unique and essential features. For Luguetti et al. (2017), the critical elements for their pedagogical model for working with socially vulnerable youth were an ethic of care, student-centred pedagogy, inquiry-based education centred in action, attentiveness to the community and community of sport. Oliver and Kirk (2015) also listed student-centred pedagogy and inquiry-based education centred in action as two of four critical elements for a pedagogical model for working with adolescent girls, the other two being pedagogies of embodiment and listening to respond over time. Four critical elements for Williams and Wainwright's (2016) model for outdoor adventure education were mainly outdoors, experiential learning, challenge by choice and managed risk.

In our earlier work (Hastie & Casey, 2014; Kirk, 2013) we referred to the critical elements as the "non-negotiables" when we were in conversation with teachers. This language was intended to clarify the purpose of the critical elements, but some readers have found it misleading and have assumed the critical elements are prescriptions for practice. For example, Landi, Fitzpatrick, and McGlashan (2016, p. 3), although referring to Metzler's benchmarks, wrote the benchmarks position "the teacher's role in the instructional process . . . to reproduce particular benchmarks that have been previously designed without knowledge of the school, students, or context." This has never been our intention, nor do we believe it is Metzler's. We have written elsewhere (Goodyear, Casey, & Kirk, 2012) that the critical elements are "non-negotiable" in so far as they must be present in the school physical education program planning and development process *in some* form, but that they will almost certainly look different in different contexts. So, for example, two teachers could develop a unit of sport education in their respective schools based on Siedentop's (1994) model, but using different sports, allocating different roles, configuring the season in specific ways, incorporating festivity using various strategies, and so on. Each of these critical elements (of sport, roles, seasons and festivity) should be sufficiently present to be discernible to the informed observer, but do not need to be the same.

Indeed, in this context, Hastie and Casey (2014) have provided advice to researchers on how they might report the fidelity of school-based practice to the pedagogical models used to construct school programs. This is important, since without some means of demonstrating the extent to which a school-based program is faithful to the practice architectures of pedagogical models, it is impossible to know whether any educational benefits in terms of student learning can be attributed to the model. Of course, teachers are at liberty to pick and choose whichever features of pedagogical models they wish to implement in their school physical education programs. But they must then be careful how they make claims about the usefulness or otherwise of any model they may have cannibalised. Casey, MacPhail, Larsson, and Quennerstedt (2020) "believe that physical education research and practice has come to see them [pedagogical models] as . . . proper nouns (words that describe a particular person, place or thing). In this way, a Model (such as Sport Education) becomes one specific thing." This "proper nouning" of models is the antithesis of fidelity and returns us to the idea that models are prescriptions for practice: something we wholeheartedly distance ourselves from.

Of course, the need for incorporation of the critical elements of pedagogical models into program planning and development at school or district level is based on the assumption that the learning aspirations stated for a given model are more likely to be realised than if the critical elements are, in part or wholly, ignored. This is an empirical question that can and should be tested in practice, a point that leads us to the next key characteristic of pedagogical models, which is that they are not prescriptions but design specifications for practice.

Before doing so, we should note that some older and well-established models such as sport education and teaching games for understanding do not have the practice architectures we have just outlined. That said, both models have been analysed by Metzler (2017) who has investigated their foundations, teaching and learning features, and implementation needs and modifications. More recently developed models, such as those referred to above (e.g. Luguetti et al., 2017; Williams & Wainwright, 2016; Oliver & Kirk, 2015) and others (e.g. Aggerholm, Standal, Barker, & Larsson, 2018), have begun to adopt the practice architectures described here as prototype models are developed and tested in practice. Kirk (2017) has also revisited the teaching games for understanding approach and begun the process of identifying practice architectures specific to the notion of MbP we are developing here, in terms of the *sayings*, *doings* and *relatings* of a main idea, critical elements and learning aspirations.

Pedagogical models as design specifications

A common misconception of pedagogical models is that they are programs in and of themselves. Even a cursory glance at sport education (Siedentop, 1994) and teaching games for understanding (Bunker & Thorpe, 1982) reveals that this is not so. In each of these well-known and frequently used approaches to physical education, only broad guiding principles are provided. While Siedentop lists three main learning aspirations (competent, literate and enthusiastic sports people), these take different forms in the versions of sport education developed by his colleague-teachers and set out in the 1994 book. Similarly, Bunker and Thorpe's "model" is actually an attempt to represent the main components of games lessons and their sequencing, so that sport techniques are not the first consideration for teachers, as is the case in multi-activity, sports technique-based approaches. Instead, sport techniques only come after the game form, game concept, and decision-making are considered.

Jewett and Bain's (1985) illustration (see Figure 2.1) makes clear our point that models are not programs *per se*, but rather design specifications that form the basis for the development of local programs. It is worth highlighting a number of features of this diagram, since it illustrates very well

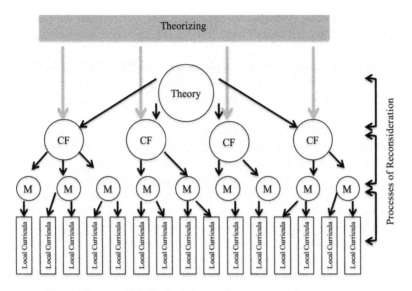

Key: CF = Conceptual Framework, M= Model

Figure 2.1   The process of model development (Jewett & Bain, 1995) [Processes of reconsideration added by Casey (2016, p. 59)]

the notion of MbP we are proposing. First, Jewett and Bain were advocating a multi-model approach to physical education. Their diagram shows that any given model might form the basis for developing one or more local school programs, making our point that models are specifications for practice, not prescriptions, and that local programs based on any one model may look different from each other. Second, each of the models is informed by what Jewett and Bain describe as "conceptual frameworks," which themselves construct and constitute "theory." It is an important feature of MbP that each model is embedded in and informed by broader theoretical perspectives on physical education's educational purposes and benefits (Kirk, 2013). Indeed, this feature is common across most advocacies for a models-based approach to physical education. Third, Casey (2016) made an addition to Jewett and Bain's diagram to highlight a point which we think was implicit in their writing but not rendered clearly in the diagram. The diagram as it is constructed in their 1985 book appears to suggest a one-way process of program planning and development, from theorist to practitioner. Following Stenhouse (1975) and his notion of "curriculum-as-specification," there is what Casey described here as processes of reconsideration, when a pedagogical model meets physical education practice. Models are constructed, not only through the ruminations of scholars, but also through testing, reflection and revision in practice contexts.

Underpinning the notion that pedagogical models – as discussed in Chapter 1 – are design specifications for practice is Stenhouse's concept of "curriculum-as-specification." Stenhouse wrote:

> Educational ideas expressed in books are not easily taken into possession by teachers, whereas the expression of ideas as curricular specifications exposes them to testing by teachers and hence establishes an equality of discourse between the proposer and those who assess his (sic) proposal. The idea is that of an educational science in which each classroom is a laboratory, each teacher a member of the scientific community. There is, of course, no implication as to the origin of the proposal or hypothesis being tested. The originator may be a classroom teacher, a policy-maker or an educational research worker. The crucial point is that the proposal is not to be regarded as an unqualified recommendation but rather a provisional specification claiming no more that to be worth putting to the test of practice. Such proposals claim to be intelligent rather than correct. I have identified a curriculum as a particular form of specification about the practice of teaching and not as a package of materials or a syllabus of ground to be covered. It is a way of translating any educational idea into a hypothesis testable in practice. It invites critical testing rather than acceptance.
>
> (Stenhouse, 1975, p. 142)

Pedagogical models, as we intend them to be understood, are design specifications for the development of programs and practice in local contexts. As such they can be considered, in Stenhouse's terms, as "a way of translating any educational idea into a hypothesis testable in practice." Models are always prototypes until they are tested in practice, reflected upon and revised, and indeed remain open to further testing and adaptation even when a critical mass of research begins to build, as in the case for example of sport education and teaching games for understanding. This is because circumstances change over time. Even for well-established models ongoing revision will always be necessary, as part of a process of sustainable renewal of physical education programs.

Clearly, pedagogical models as design specifications need to be robust enough to stand the tests of practice, providing teachers and other members of school communities such as students with sufficient guidance to be able to create their own local curricula. The practice architectures of pedagogical models need to provide just enough guidance to generate quality physical education programs without prescribing in detail what teachers and students should do. We recognise that in order to achieve this balance the process of developing new prototype pedagogical models needs to be done in partnership, ideally as a collaborative process between researchers, curriculum developers, school practitioners and students.

This is one important reason why pedagogical models need to be developed in partnership. But it is not the only one. We know from curriculum research over many years that it is not possible, nor desirable, to exclude teachers, students and other local stakeholders from the process of program planning and development and expect genuine curriculum innovation and quality programs to result. Pedagogical models as design specifications are intended to provide one means of managing the inevitable and unavoidable tension between local agency and external support.

Managing the tension between local agency and external support

It has been a fantasy of a particular school of curriculum developers since the 1960s to "teacher-proof" curricula so that the intentions of the developers can impact students directly, without any mediation, refraction or distortion by teachers. At the present time, the prevalence of high stakes testing arguably keeps this fantasy alive. But some educational policymakers soon saw that this aspiration was not only insulting to teachers, but was also impossible to realise. Why, in any case, would an educational jurisdiction employ teachers in schools and then seek to bypass them? As the work of Stenhouse and colleagues showed, teachers are essential contributors to the educational process, and thus their professional learning and developing experience and expertise are of paramount importance.

More than this, as Kirk and Macdonald's (2001) concept of the "local context of implementation" and more recently Priestley, Edwards, Priestley, and Miller's (2012) "spaces for manoeuvre" show, teachers play a decisive and inevitable part in the translation of educational ideas into practice. Educational innovation obeys an "iron law," that the innovative idea will always and inevitably be transformed in the process of implementation. Kirk and Macdonald (2001) argued that there are at least two "moments" in this process of transformation. The first is when a teacher meets a new idea and attempts to make sense of it in relation to their own biography of experience, and their own understanding of their field of expertise. The second is when they take this understanding to their workplace and attempt to adapt and shape it to fit their schools, their programs, their students and their own preferences, beliefs and tastes. Priestley et al. (2012) argued that there is nothing necessarily benign about this process. Teachers may translate ideas positively and accurately or negatively and incorrectly, or indeed may seek to sabotage their own implementation.

Nevertheless, transformation in the process of implementation is inevitable, not just at this level of programs and teachers, but also between teachers and their students. Amade-Escot (2007, p. 16), writing about the French concept of *la transposition didactique*, revealed a second process of transformation wherein teachers and students, as an intrinsic part of their educational interactions, both reconfigure and co-construct knowledge. Indeed, this notion of reconfiguration and co-construction of knowledge within the pedagogic relationship of teachers and students is a key feature of activist pedagogy in physical education (Oliver & Kirk, 2015) and other critical pedagogies (Kirk, 2020). We come back to this issue of co-construction of physical educational knowledge below.

Accepting the inevitable participation, interaction and influence of teachers and students in educational action is an important first step in the program planning and development process. Through their practice architectures, pedagogical models seek to manage the tension inherent in the relationships between local agency and external support. The main idea, critical elements and statement of learning aspirations, and alignment of curriculum, teaching, learning, and assessment provide the support for teachers and students to create programs that best fit their local contexts. Consistent with Stenhouse's (1975, p. 144) concept of curriculum-as-specification, teachers are viewed as "extended professionals" who have "a capacity for autonomous professional self-development through a systematic self-study, through the study of the work of other teachers and through the testing of ideas by classroom research procedures." While Stenhouse stressed the notion of "teacher-as-researcher," it is clear that he saw this work as part of a wider configuration of collaborating educational professionals such as policy-makers, developers and researchers, and other stakeholders, including parents and students.

Researchers, in this context, have opportunities to provide school communities with a variety of forms of support. One of these is the creation and development of pedagogical models in prototype form, educational ideas that are testable in practice and capable of translation into practice. Researchers also have opportunities to support the work of school communities through the provision of professional learning experiences, which could include the development of research skills. Certainly, they have the means, through scholarly publications, to spread the word about ideas that are worth putting to the test of practice and that have been shown to work. They also have the means to carry out research with teachers and students in order to develop local programs and the models that inform them, and to begin to create a critical mass of knowledge about them. This is not to suggest that pedagogical models can only be produced by researchers, nor that they have sole access to research and scholarly writing skills. But they do have capabilities and capacities to work with school communities to develop quality physical education programs, and as a resource are generally underused in many educational systems.

Conclusion

In this chapter we have highlighted the high degree of commonality that we see amongst scholars' and practitioners' intentions when working with the notion of models and MBP. That being said, we also argued that "true MBP does not yet exist" (Casey, 2014, p. 30). We reasoned, however, that without adopting a multi-model approach and positioning pedagogical models as organising centres for physical education programmes, MbP could not exist. Subsequently, and in keeping with the nature of a book of this kind, we reasoned that any proposal we made for MbP must therefore be theoretical until such times as multi-model programs are in place in schools.

It is our belief that MbP could work to benefit all students. Each model has its own practice architectures of *sayings*, *doings* and *relatings*, of main idea, critical elements and learning aspirations. In envisioning MbP, we posited that whatever is said about a model, what is done in a gymnasium or classroom with a model, and the functions and rules of the school or subject, might both enable and constrain model implementation.

By aligning curriculum, teaching, learning and assessment and by acknowledging and utilising the local context of implementation that exists within both schools and the pedagogical relationship between teachers and students, we see the potential of MbP to reform physical education as fair, inclusive and equitable. In this chapter we distance ourselves from the idea "the teacher's role in the instructional process . . . [is] to reproduce particular benchmarks that have been previously designed without knowledge of the school, students, or context" (Landi et al., 2016, p. 3). Instead, we argue that each model has its own critical elements which, through providing each model with its own distinctive architectures, almost certainly look different in different contexts. This is fundamental in our conceptualisation of MbP. Models are not one thing. They are "spaces for manoeuvre" where transformation of innovative ideas during the process of implementation is both inevitable and desirable.

In the next three chapters we explore the practice architectures of a number of pedagogical models from the macro perspective of model-makers and advocates (Chapter 3), the meso perspective of literature reviewers (Chapter 4) and the micro perspective of individual empirical studies (Chapter 5). In doing so we seek to view the practice of models, through the different scales envisioned by Kemmis (2019) i.e. the macro (in our case the models themselves), through the meso of our conduct with a model (i.e. the literature of single model MBP), through to the "moment-by-moment talk and interaction that unfolds in practices as they are performed" (p. 13). Moreover, we seek to understand how the main idea, critical elements, learning aspirations and pedagogy of different models encounter the world, the people and the practice of physical education.

References

Aggerholm, K., Standal, O., Barker, D. M., & Larsson, H. (2018). On practising in physical education: Outline for a pedagogical model. *Physical Education and Sport Pedagogy*, *23*(2), 197–208.

Amade-Escot, C. (2000). The contribution of two research programs on teaching content: "Pedagogical content knowledge" and "didactics of physical education". *Journal of Teaching Physical Education*, *20*(1), 78–101.

Amade-Escot, C. (2007). *Le Didactique*. Paris: Edition Revue EPS.

Bunker, D., & Thorpe, R. (1982). A model for the teaching of games in the secondary school. *Bulletin of Physical Education*, *10*, 9–16.

Casey, A. (2014). Models-based practice: Great white hope or white elephant? *Physical Education and Sport Pedagogy*, *19*(1), 18–34.

Casey, A. (2016). Models-based practice. In C. D. Ennis (Ed.), *Routledge handbook of physical education pedagogies* (pp. 54–67). London: Routledge.

Casey, A., & Dyson, B. (2009). The implementation of models-based practice in physical education through action research. *European Physical Education Review*, *15*(2), 175–199.

Casey, A., & MacPhail, A. (2018). Adopting a models-based approach to teaching physical education. *Physical Education and Sport Pedagogy*, *23*(3), 294–310.

Casey, A., MacPhail, A., Larsson, H., & Quennerstedt, M. (2020). Between hope and happening: Problematizing the M and the P in models-based practice. *Physical Education and Sport Pedagogy*. https://doi.org/10.1080/17408989.2020.1789576.

Cothran, D. J., & Kulinna, P. (2008). Teachers' knowledge about and use of teaching models. *The Physical Educator*, *65*(3), 122–133.

Dudley, D., Goodyear, V. A., & Baxter, D. (2016). Quality and health-optimizing physical education: Using assessment at the health and education nexus. *Journal of Teaching in Physical Education*, *35*, 324–366.

Dyson, B., Kulinna, P., & Metzler, M. (2016). Introduction to the special issue: Models-based practice in physical education. *Journal of Teaching in Physical Education*, *35*, 297–298.

Goodyear, V. A., Casey, A., & Kirk, D. (2012). Hiding behind the camera: Social learning within the cooperative learning model to engage girls in physical education. *Sport, Education and Society, 19*(6), 712–734.

Goodyear, V. A., Casey, A., & Kirk, D. (2017). Practice architectures and sustainable curriculum renewal. *Journal of Curriculum Studies, 49*(2), 235–254.

Gurvitch, R., Lund, J. L., & Metzler, M. W. (2008). Chapter 1: Researching the adoption of model-based instruction – context and chapter summaries. *Journal of Teaching in Physical Education, 27*, 449–456.

Haerens, L., Kirk, D., Cardon, G., & De Bourdeaudhuij, I. (2011). Toward the development of a pedagogical model for health-based physical education. *Quest, 63*(3), 321–338.

Hastie, P. A., & Casey, A. (2014). Fidelity in models-based practice research in sport pedagogy: A guide for future investigations. *Journal of Teaching in Physical Education, 33*, 422–431.

Hopmann, S. (2007). Restrained teaching: The common core of didaktik. *European Educational Research Journal, 6*(2), 109–124.

Jewett, A. E., & Bain, L. L. (1985). *The curriculum process in physical education*. Dubuque, IA: Wm. C. Brown.

Jewett, A. E., Bain, L. L., & Ennis, C. (1995). *The curriculum process in physical education* (2nd ed.). Dubuque, IA: Wm. C. Brown.

Joyce, B., & Weil, M. (1980). *Models of teaching* (2nd ed.). Englewood Cliffs, NJ: Prentice Hall.

Kemmis, S. (2018). *Educational research and the good for humankind: Changing education to secure a sustainable world*. Keynote address at the seminar Education, Fatherland and Humanity, University of Jyväskylä, Finland. Retrieved June 1, 2020, from https://ktl.jyu.fi/en/current/news/180524-ed-research-and-the-good_23.pdf

Kemmis, S. (2019). *A practice sensibility: An invitation to the theory of practice architectures*. Singapore: Springer.

Kemmis, S., & Grootenboer, P. (2008). Situating praxis in practice: Practice architectures and the cultural, social and material conditions for practice. In S. Kemmis & T. J. Smith (Eds.), *Enabling praxis: Challenges for education* (pp. 37–62). Rotterdam: Sense.

Kemmis, S., Wilkinson, J., Edwards-Groves, C., Hardy, I., Grootenboer, P., & Bristol, L. (2014). *Changing practices, changing education*. London: Springer.

Kirk, D. (1990). *Educacion fisica y curriculum: Introduccion critica*. Valencia: Universitat de Valencia.

Kirk, D. (2013). Educational value and models-based practice in physical education. *Educational Philosophy and Theory, 45*(9), 973–986.

Kirk, D. (2017). Teaching games in physical education: Towards a pedagogical model. *Revista Portuguesa de Ciencias do Desporto, 17*(S1.A), 17–26.

Kirk, D. (2020). *Precarity, critical pedagogy and physical education*. London: Routledge.

Kirk, D., Lamb, C. A., Oliver, K. L., Ewing-Day, R., Fleming, C., Loch, A., & Smedley, V. (2018). Balancing prescription with teacher and pupil agency: Spaces for manoeuvre within a pedagogical model for working with adolescent girls. *The Curriculum Journal, 29*(2), 219–237.

Kirk, D., & MacDonald, D. (2001). Teacher voice and ownership of curriculum change. *Journal of Curriculum Studies, 33*(5), 551–567.

Landi, D., Fitzpatrick, K., & McGlashan, H. (2016). Models based practices in physical education: A sociocritical reflection. *Journal of Teaching in Physical Education, 35*(4), 400–411.

Luguetti, C., Oliver, K. L., Dantas, L., & Kirk, D. (2017). "The life of crime does not pay; stop and think!": The process of co-constructing a prototype pedagogical model of sport for working with youth from socially vulnerable backgrounds. *Physical Education and Sport Pedagogy, 22*(4), 329–348.

Lund, J., & Tannehill, D. (2014). *Standards-based physical education curriculum development* (3rd ed.). Burlington, MA: Jones & Bartlett Publishers.

Metzler, M. W. (2000). *Instructional models for physical education*. Needham Heights, MA: Allyn and Bacon.

Metzler, M. W. (2017). *Instructional models for physical education* (3rd ed.). London: Routledge.

Oliver, K. L., & Kirk, D. (2015). *Girls, gender and physical education: An activist approach*. New York: Routledge.

Priestley, M., Edwards, R., Priestley, A., & Miller, K. (2012). Teacher agency in curriculum-making: Agents of change and spaces for manoeuvre. *Curriculum Inquiry, 42*(2), 191–214.

Schatzki, T. R. (2002). *The site of the social: A philosophical account of the constitution of social life and change*. University Park, PA: University of Pennsylvania Press.

Siedentop, D. (1994). *Sport education: Quality PE through positive sport experiences*. Champaign, IL: Human Kinetics.

Siedentop, D. (1996). Valuing the physically active life: Contemporary and future directions. *Quest, 48*(3), 266–274.

Siedentop, D., & Tannehill, D. (2000). *Developing teaching skills in physical education* (4th ed.). Mountain View, CA: Mayfield Publishing Company.

Stenhouse, L. (1975). *An introduction to curriculum research and development*. London: Heinemann.

Williams, A., & Wainwright, N. (2016). A new pedagogical model for adventure in the curriculum: Part two – outlining the model. *Physical Education and Sport Pedagogy, 21*(6), 589–602.

3 The practice architectures of pedagogical models

Introduction

We noted in Chapter 2 that the notion of MbP is contested. We also noted that this contested term, and related notions such as MBI and MBP, appear regularly and interchangeably in the scholarly literature. Furthermore, we explored the uses of terms such as curriculum models and instructional models and argued for our preferred concept of pedagogical models. These are not the only contested notions in the research literature. The very idea of applying the descriptor "pedagogical model" to some important and well-established approaches to physical education has only limited consensus among the scholarly and practice communities and, indeed, among the originators of these approaches themselves. It is the case that neither Siedentop for sport education, nor Bunker and Thorpe for teaching games for understanding, nor Hellison for teaching personal and social responsibility, described their approaches as pedagogical models. However, in further developing our rationale for MbP in this and the following chapters, we propose to do just that.

We will do so by mapping the main features, pedagogical purposes and development of several approaches to physical education through the lenses of the three sets of arrangements of practice architectures we outlined in Chapter 2. In doing so we take up the invitation to:

> explore how practices are shaped by cultural-discursive [*sayings*], material-economic [*doings*] and socio-political [*relatings*] conditions – conditions that are present, and, as we have seen, conditions that may be absent. It invites us to explore how we develop the practices we do by being interlocutors in particular settings, by being embodied persons moving among other people and objects in those places, and by being social beings responding to the different kinds of conditions of power and solidarity found there. It also invites us to consider how practices

adapt and change in response to changing conditions, and how changes can be for better or for worse.

(Kemmis, 2019, p. 19, original emphasis)

Through this analysis, we seek to establish the extent to which it is possible for each of these approaches to physical education to identify a main idea, critical elements and learning aspirations. We also want to investigate possible alignment of curriculum, teaching and learning in the pursuit and realisation of specific and distinctive learning aspirations. On this latter point (about the distinctiveness of specific pedagogical models in terms of their signature practice architectures) we are interested in searching for overlapping or common features of models as well as their unique aspects. The point of this chapter is, therefore, to establish the feasibility of describing some well-established forms of physical education as pedagogical models and, as such, as core components of MbP. We suggested in Chapter 2 that pedagogical models have these features as key aspects of their practice architectures, expressed in *sayings*, *doings* and *relatings*.

Main Idea: The main purpose and character of a model.

Critical Elements: Provide a pedagogical model with its distinctive "shape" as well as giving users some sense of what the creators of the model regard as its unique and essential features.

Learning Aspirations: Relate specifically to the main idea or theme of the model. In contrast to multi-activity, sport technique-based approaches, where learning "outcomes" are often specified across several domains, learning aspirations involve differentiation in learning tasks, teaching styles and assessment practices.

Pedagogy: The alignment of the four features pedagogy (i.e. the interacting and interdependent elements of curriculum, teaching, learning and assessment) is of utmost importance in pedagogical models and is the feature that is often lacking in traditional practice.

We consider, in turn, the practice architectures of sport education, game-centred approaches, cooperative learning, teaching personal and social responsibility, and activist approaches to physical education. In this chapter, we go to the writing of the originators of each of these approaches, where they are identifiable, to search for and identify the *sayings*, *doings* and *relatings* of each approach. In short, we are seeking to understand the ways in which the practice of MbP, through the pedagogical model as a foundational element, is prefigured (Schatzki, 2002) by the writing of the originators. Importantly, even though these originators may not have described their approaches as pedagogical models, our question here is whether they might, nevertheless, through this analysis of practice architectures, be reconceptualised as pedagogical models. Ultimately, we seek to understand what practices look like, how teachers might conceptualise and enact a MbP approach to physical education, and suggest some sustainable approaches to MbP.

Sport education

In writing his own retrospective of sport education, Siedentop (2002) explored the origins of the model. Built on the play education element of his doctoral thesis, and its development through his leadership of a programme of doctoral research at Ohio State University, sport education was first revealed to the physical education and sport pedagogy community in Siedentop's keynote address at the Commonwealth Games Conference in Brisbane, Australia (Siedentop, 1982). Much of the early work presented in this address sought to explore the *sayings* of physical education and of sport in an effort to "provide the model's ultimate justification" (Siedentop, 1982, p. 3). The main thrust of Siedentop's argument was that competition was not properly understood or enacted in physical education. Basing his argument on two underlying assumptions, Siedentop held that sport derives its meaning from play as a ludic activity (what Caillois (1961, p. 32) described as "the primitive desire to find diversion and amusement"). Following this assertion to its conclusion, he maintained that sport, and therefore sport education, "represents an evolution of culture towards a more meaningful form, one which will tend to contribute to the culture's growth and survival" (p. 3). He argued that his assumptions were markedly different from others arguing for the place of sport in society. In his words "what [he] want[ed] to argue goes something like this" (p. 4):

If sport is an institutional form of higher ludic activity; if sport is equal in value to other ludic forms, both for the individual and the culture; and if more appropriate participation in sport by more people represents a positive step in cultural evolution; then sport education is justified as a conceptual model of what we do. Indeed, it is not only justified but its importance to mankind (sic) is seen more clearly through this set of assumptions and, subsequently, its proper place in education is more secure. I am arguing for a sport culture that is both sane and exciting – sport in all its form for all the people – recognising that for some of the people the appropriate form is what we refer to as elite sport. I am also arguing for sport as a basic subject matter in the education of children and youth sport and as a fundamental activity in society.

(Siedentop, 1982, p. 4)

It would be easy to argue that Siedentop was making a broader argument about the place of sport in the *sayings*, *doings* and *relatings* of our culture but the arguments he makes are aspirational and, as such, should be considered as semantic, i.e. as *sayings*. He works in the semantic space because it allows him to build a case for sport education. In presenting, for the first time, his fundamental argument for sport education he argues for what we now recognise as radical reform (Kirk, 2010) in both physical education's detrimental treatment of sport as the potential antithesis of education and society's opinion of sport as a cruder form of ludic activity.

Having done this, Siedentop (1982, p. 4) conceptualises the main characteristic of sport education as "education in sport" and, for the first time, sets out what we see as an early articulation of the main idea of sport education (see table 3.1) i.e. "to develop players, in the fullest and richest sense of the meaning of that term" (Siedentop, 1982, p. 4). To do this, and in doing so engage in higher forms of ludic activity, he argues that players should:

- practice
- defer gratification
- gain a taste for imposed difficulty
- subordinate themselves to the rules
- engage in increasing complex strategy
- observe ritual, and
- appreciate the traditions of sport.

Siedentop envisioned that the significant *doings* of an education in sport should involve competition which, in its fullest sense, "involves tradition, ritual, celebration, intimacy, and the sharing of significant experiences" (p. 4). He compared this richness of competition to school practice and held that

> organising a game in a physical education class at the end of a three week unit does not do justice to the festive nature of competition – and it is the festival nature of competition that provides one of its most sustaining sources of motivation.
>
> (Siedentop, 1982, p. 4)

In these statements we begin to see the emergence of the critical elements and learning aspirations of sport education, although they are not fully articulated until later iterations of the model (see Siedentop, Mand, & Taggart, 1986; Siedentop, 1994; Siedentop, Hastie, & van der Mars, 2004).

The *relatings* pertaining to sport education at its birth in 1982 and its place in education revolve around developmental appropriateness. Siedentop

(1982, p. 5) voiced a now well-rehearsed argument that children should not be playing adult games:

> Imposing complex parent games on children is akin to asking a child to read a novel with a complex plot. These are ways to turn children off good sport and good literature. The result is a society in which the literature levels gradually diminish.

He went further:

> It is not just that inappropriate programs in the early years produce children who do not read well or children who are motorically illiterate, although that clearly is a problem. The larger problem is a society in which adults consume literature that is, at best, mediocre – literature that demeans rather than strengthens the culture. So, too, do adults participate in sport, often casually and in ways that are not terribly meaningful. Reading an occasional junk paperback is akin to participating in an occasional pick-up softball game – it has the look of the real thing but lacks substance and it's difficult to describe as growth enhancing either for the individual or the culture.
>
> (Siedentop, 1982, p. 5)

At the crux of his argument was the idea that sport education was designed for the betterment of society, inasmuch that it could meet society's need for higher forms of ludic activity in ways that pick-up games couldn't. In an attempt to utilise the importance of sport in some cultures, Siedentop (1982) argued that sport as traditionally practised in physical education was neither exciting nor important in the grander scheme of schooling or life. He argued, therefore, that it should relate more to the best features of sports culture. In short, "sport education might . . . develop sport forms, sport participation, and sport spectatorship in ways that helps the culture to grow in positive directions rather than to decline" (Siedentop, 1982, p. 7). Whilst many of these arguments had disappeared by the time his seminal *Sport Education: quality PE through Positive Sport Experiences* book was published (Siedentop, 1994), he was still arguing that there are too many barriers to meaningful participation in sport:

> If 'Sport in all its forms for all the people' is a worthy ethic, then physical educators – in their roles of sport educators – have the potential to become the grass roots guardians of a healthy, sane, participatory sport culture.
>
> (Siedentop, 1994, p. 6)

Having considered, and retrofitted, practice architectures to sport education we see foundational arguments that position sport as culturally important, whilst seriously questioning the cultural relevance of parent games, pick-up games and physical education. What we also see is the emergence of what we have named the main idea, critical elements, learning aspirations and pedagogy of sport education. Tracing these through four practitioner-facing papers and books (Siedentop, 1982; Siedentop et al., 1986; Siedentop, 1994; Siedentop et al., 2004) we not only see the genesis of these constructs but also their evolution (see Table 3.1). In what remains of this section we will explore these concepts.

Whilst the main idea of sport education has evolved, Siedentop (1982, p. 4) laid its enduring foundation in Brisbane when he stated that the model set out "to develop players, in the fullest and richest sense of the meaning of that term." In *Physical education: teaching and curriculum strategies for grades 5–12*, Siedentop et al. (1986) introduced sports education to the scholarly community and, in doing so, modified the language of the main idea. "Players" became "students" and "develop" became "teach" perhaps in a reflection of the participants and subject matter of physical education. By 1994, Siedentop had added "educate" at the start and coins the term "competent, literate and enthusiastic sportspersons" now so synonymous with the model. In fact, it could be argued that the latter part of the statement has replaced the former in the literature around sport education. It is certainly the goal of sport education put forward by Siedentop et al. (2004).

Whilst the critical elements have been less scrutinised across the final three texts than in his 1986 text, they are absent in Siedentop's Commonwealth Games keynote. Siedentop et al. (1986, p. 186) introduced them by asking "what characterizes sport as an institutionalized form of motor play, and how does sport differ from the ways in which physical education is typically organised and implemented?" Siedentop and his co-authors went on to define these characteristics as seasons, affiliation, formal competition, culminating events, and records. In 1994 Siedentop added festivity, whilst modifying events to the singular event and records to keeping records.

Tracking the evolution of sport education's learning aspirations is more convoluted as they aren't articulated so clearly in the various texts. In 1982, Siedentop explored the evolution of play beyond:

> diversion, spontaneity, turbulence and other elements so clear in the play of little children . . . [to explore] meaning derive[d] from the higher characteristics of ludic activity.
>
> (Siedentop, 1982, p. 12)

Table 3.1 The main idea, critical elements and learning aspirations of sport education

Main Idea	Critical Elements	Learning Aspirations
"To develop players, in the fullest and richest sense of the meaning of that term" (Siedentop, 1982, p. 4)	Seasons (Siedentop et al., 1986; Siedentop, 1994; Siedentop et al., 2004)	**Competent** Practice (Siedentop, 1982; Siedentop et al., 1986). Develop sport-specific techniques and fitness (Siedentop, 1994; Siedentop et al., 2004) Share planning and administration of sport experiences (Siedentop, 1994; Siedentop et al., 2004)
"To teach them [students] to be players, in the fullest sense of that term" (Siedentop et al., 1986, p. 186)	Affiliation (Siedentop et al., 1986; Siedentop, 1994; Siedentop et al., 2004)	Participate at a developmentally appropriate level (Siedentop, 1994; Siedentop et al., 2004)
"To educate students to be players in the fullest sense and help them to develop as competent, literate and enthusiastic sportspersons" (Siedentop, 1994; Siedentop et al., 2004, p. 7)	Formal Competition (Siedentop et al., 1986; Siedentop, 1994; Siedentop et al., 2004)	**Literate** The adoption of specific roles (Siedentop, 1982; Siedentop et al., 1986). Provide responsible leadership (Siedentop, 1994; Siedentop et al., 2004) Develop the capacity to make reasoned decisions about sport concerns (Siedentop, 1994; Siedentop et al., 2004) Subordination to rules (Siedentop, 1982). Develop and apply knowledge about umpiring, refereeing and training (Siedentop, 1994; Siedentop et al., 2004)
	Culminating events (Siedentop et al., 1986) Culmination Event (Siedentop, 1994; Siedentop et al., 2004)	Increasing complexity both in strategy and performance (Siedentop, 1982; Siedentop et al., 1986). Appreciate and be able to execute sport-specific strategic play (Siedentop, 1994; Siedentop et al., 2004)
	Records (Siedentop et al., 1986) Keeping Records (Siedentop, 1994) Record Keeping (Siedentop et al., 2004, p. 6)	**Enthusiastic** The observance of ritual, and an appreciation for tradition (Siedentop, 1982; Siedentop et al., 1986). Appreciate the rituals and conventions that give sports their unique meanings (Siedentop, 1994; Siedentop et al., 2004) Work effectively within a group toward common goals (Siedentop, 1994; Siedentop et al., 2004)
	Festivity (Siedentop, 1994; Siedentop et al., 2004)	Become involved in sport after school and outside of school (Siedentop, 1994; Siedentop et al., 2004)

By 1986, these learning aspirations were explained as "mature forms of play" that "require practice, sustained involvement, the learning of specific skills, the understanding of rules and strategies, and an appreciation for the customs and traditions of the play form" (Siedentop et al., 1986, p. 190). By 1994 these are articulated as the "immediate and comprehensive objectives" (Siedentop, 1994, p. 4) of sport education seen in Table 3.1. In their *Complete guide to sport education*, Siedentop et al. (2004) positioned the same, now short-term, objectives of sport education as vehicles for achieving the long-term goals (what we have positioned as the main idea and critical elements of the model).

The pedagogy of sport education originates in play theory. Primarily, Siedentop (1982, p. 5) aspired to a "gradual socialisation from the characteristics of lower forms of ludic activity – namely turbulence, gaiety, spontaneity – to the characteristics of higher forms of ludic activity." Interestingly, Siedentop's expertise in behaviourism can be seen in the first iteration of the model. Contrasting contemporaneous physical education with the pursuit of sport, he asked:

> How many of us are grown accustomed to using terms such as the whole child, the active learner, individual differences, and a meaningful curriculum when we discuss physical education? So, too, most of us shy away from using terms such as rote learning, indoctrination, memorisation, and even training. Such are the polemical ghosts that we accept without thought when we discuss physical education. Yet in sport we feel quite willing to discuss training, and the repeated practice of fundamentals is seen as a necessary task even for the most advanced performers.
>
> (Siedentop, 1982, p. 5)

Consequently, it is hard to pin down the pedagogical expectations of sport education. Siedentop et al. (1986, p. 200) highlight the importance of practice to help "students improve their skills, their abilities to play sports, and their attitudes towards sports participation." At the same time they use terminology like "task-reoriented" and ask "coaches," who may be physical education teachers, to improve "students' individual abilities and their group abilities to communicate" (p. 200). In his 1994 book, Siedentop has better defined the role of teachers as "the architects of the educational environment and the persons who are ultimately responsible for its efficiency and vitality" (p. 15). He begins by positioning the teacher as a planner and a manager before arguing that:

> Because values and fair play are so central to sport education, you must above all explain, model, and provide purposeful practice for good

sporting behaviour, not in the abstract, nor on a written test, but when it counts, during competition itself. Values and attitudes are formed slowly and need to be attended to consistently. This requires that you design an educational environment where fair play and sporting values are taught, practised, and reinforce consistently.

(Siedentop, 1994, p. 15)

Twenty years later, Siedentop et al. (2004) detailed the key instructional features of sport education, i.e. detailed practice, independent practice, and technique practice, and draw on other pedagogical models such as play practice, game sense and tactical games to support the teacher in their new role.

Sport education has evolved into the model that we now see in research and practitioner literatures. There is, however, and as we will explore in Chapters 4 and 5, a difference between the practice architectures, main idea, critical elements, learning aspirations and pedagogy articulated by Siedentop and colleagues and the actualisation of the model in practice. Since Siedentop, as we noted, did not conceptualise sport education as a pedagogical model, there is some uncertainty around identifying the main idea and learning aspirations of sport education. In our view, the notion of competent, literate and enthusiastic learners could be thought of usefully as the learning aspirations of sport education as a pedagogical model as well as the main idea. Consequently, we have presented these as subheadings in Table 3.1 and argue that any user of sport education would enjoy "space to manoeuvre" in their ambition to achieve these aspirations.

Game-centred approaches

Arguably, Bunker and Thorpe's (1982) creation, teaching games for under-standing, was the first formulation of what we are calling Game-Centred Approaches (GCAs) in the Anglophone community. This said, Grehaigne (1989) argued that a similar approach in the Francophone community, developed in the 1970s, predated teaching games for understanding. This approach informed his and other Francophone researchers work on teaching and learning in team games prior to its meeting with the emerging Anglo-phone tradition. The tactical decision learning model (TDLM) (Grehaigne, Richard, & Griffin, 2005) was an outcome of the fusion of the Anglophone and Francophone research on games teaching and learning. This model also illustrates the proliferation of approaches to games teaching and learning since the 1980s. Here, and for the sake of brevity, we consider two GCAs. We begin with a consideration of teaching games for understanding before pondering the tactical games approach. In doing so we acknowledge both the plethora of game-centred alternatives available and the limitations imposed by keeping the chapter to a manageable length.

Teaching games for understanding

In the first chapter of Thorpe, Bunker, and Almond's (1986) seminal work *Rethinking Games Teaching*, Thorpe and Bunker (1986, p. 5) tracked the "landmarks on our way to 'teaching for understanding.'" In doing so they argued that the small-sided games, now so prevalent in their teaching games for understanding model, were originally "merely the vehicle for the transmission of skills from teacher to taught" (p. 5). Drawing on the work of two undergraduate students (Graham, 1971; Stephenson, 1972 [both mentioned but not cited by Thorpe & Bunker, 1986, p. 5]), the authors rationalised that:

> Teaching a class skills that many of them would never achieve and some had already mastered was not the equal of a modified games approach which allowed "the *game*" to develop and, what is more, allowed the teacher to assist individuals and small groups with their own technical deficiencies.
>
> (Thorpe & Bunker, 1986, p. 5, original emphasis)

In this first attempt to understand what games are about we see not only hints at the main idea of teaching games for understanding (see Table 3.2) but also its practice architectures. Fundamentally, it was the acknowledgment that understanding of games does not come from piecing different elements of established games together in physical education. Instead it comes through the relationship the learner has with the game.

This relationship (between game and learner) – what we will define later as being central to the main idea of teaching games for understanding – is built on Bunker and Thorpe's (1986) observations of games teaching. They contended that:

> present games teaching shows at best, a series of highly structured lessons leaning heavily on the teaching of techniques, or at worst lessons which rely on the children themselves to sustain interest in the game.
>
> (Bunker & Thorpe, 1986, p. 7)

This, in turn, prompted them to explore the *sayings* of physical education generally and games teaching specifically. Fundamentally, they believed games teaching had led to:

a   A large percentage of children achieving little success due to the emphasis on performance i.e. "doing"

Table 3.2 The main idea, critical elements and learning aspirations of teaching games for understanding and tactical games

Main Idea	Critical Elements	Learning Aspirations
How can we play a game? (Bunker & Thorpe, 1982) Improve students' game performance (Griffin et al., 1997)	Game Form (Bunker & Thorpe, 1982; Griffin et al., 1997)	Use game forms that align with children's age and experience (Bunker & Thorpe, 1982) Modified or conditioned games (Griffin et al., 1997)
	Game Appreciation (Bunker & Thorpe, 1982)	Understand the rules of the game to be played (Bunker & Thorpe, 1982) Understand that rules give a game its shape. They determine time and space in the game, how points are scored, and the skills required (Bunker & Thorpe, 1982). Exaggerated playing conditions (Griffin et al., 1997)
	Tactical Awareness (Bunker & Thorpe, 1982; Griffin et al., 1997)	Understand the ways and means of creating and denying space (Bunker & Thorpe, 1982). Consider tactical problems and decide on complexity of solutions (Griffin et al., 1997) Recognition of opponent(s) weakness (Bunker & Thorpe, 1982)
	Decision Making (Bunker & Thorpe, 1982)	Recognising cues and possible action outcome i.e. what to do (Bunker & Thorpe, 1982) Selecting appropriate responses i.e. how to do it (Bunker & Thorpe, 1982)
	Skill Execution (Bunker & Thorpe, 1982; Griffin et al., 1997)	Production of the required movement (always seen in the context of the learner and the game) (Bunker & Thorpe, 1982). Students apply improved skill and tactical understanding in a game (Griffin et al., 1997)
	Performance (Bunker & Thorpe, 1982)	The observed outcome of the previous processes (Bunker & Thorpe, 1982)

b   The majority of school leavers "knowing" very little about games
c   The production of supposedly "skilful" players who in fact possess inflexible techniques and poor decision-making capacity
d   The development of teacher/coach dependent performers
e   The failure to develop "thinking" spectators and "knowing" administrators at a time when games (and sport) are an important form of entertainment in the leisure industry (Bunker & Thorpe, 1986, p. 7).

Thus, the *sayings* of teaching games for understanding introduced a new vocabulary to physical education teachers around games teaching and learning. This vocabulary included terms like game form, modified games, representation and exaggeration, tactical awareness and game concept.

A focus on the *doings* of physical education as something devoid of, or at least deficient in, knowledge, skill and thought development, says much about the practice of physical education in the late 1970s and early 1980s. The focus on specific techniques (motor skills) in decontextualised practices reflects the hierarchical relationship that Bunker and Thorpe (1986) saw between the "how" of the skill and the "why" of the game. Actions, in other words, were expected to come before the potential consequences of those actions were understood. The *doings* of teaching games for understanding were thus to play a modified form of the game as a first principle, adjusted to the learners' experience and capability. This key *doing* of teaching games for understanding led some critics to claim that it eliminated technique development altogether in learning to play games. This was, however, a misleading claim, since technique development remained an essential "doing" of teaching games for understanding which was reordered in the learning process. It became something that was learned once players had begun to develop their tactical awareness and decision making using the skills they already possessed.

Given the lack of a national curriculum in England at the time teaching games for understanding was introduced, coupled with the sparseness of Bunker and Thorpe's article (limited, as it was, to four pages), it's hard to disentangle the *relatings* of the model as originally conceptualised. It must be remembered, however, that the 1980s was a time when physical education teachers had a degree of instructional and content autonomy unrecognisable today. This autonomy of curricular choice was witnessed by Whitehead and Hendry (1976, p. 11), when they set out to consider "the freedom invested by the British government in the teacher of physical education to design his or her own physical education programmes." These authors reported that physical education teachers were not required to publish syllabuses, had freedom to develop their own programmes and, as a consequence, "the tendency is for teachers to teach physical education lessons which could not necessarily be described as 'modern' or 'educational'" (Whitehead & Hendry, 1976, p. 19).

In their consideration of teachers' rules, routines, and expectations prior to and following the implementation of the *National Curriculum for Physical Education* in England in 1992, Curtner-Smith, Todorovich, Lacon, and Kerr (1999, p. 26) concluded that:

> the structural core of these teachers' managerial systems consisted of routines designed to start activity, stop activity, deal with equipment, gather pupils for demonstrations/explanations, and organise pupils for activity. Of equal importance were the expectations that pupils should learn the skills and strategies of the various activities included in the curriculum, give maximum effort, pay attention, be on-task, and be safe.

The *relatings* represented in these two examples speak to an environment where autonomy over learning, teaching, curriculum and assessment lay squarely with the teacher. Furthermore, it is indicative of a situation where this autonomy had created what has been described as THE way of teaching physical education, i.e. "physical education-as-sport-techniques" (Kirk, 2010, p. 42). Such was the apparent lack of *relatings* at national level, or even regional level, that local decision-making dominated the choices made regarding physical education; decisions that Bunker and Thorpe (1986) highlighted and railed against in their article.

The tactical games approach

In the first edition of *teaching sports concepts and skills* book, Griffin, Mitchell, and Oslin (1997) introduced their tactical approach. At the heart of the model is the main idea of "improv[ing] students' game performance, which involves combining tactical awareness and skill execution" (Griffin et al., 1997, p. 8). This main idea doesn't stray far from its foundation in Bunker and Thorpe's (1986) teaching games for understanding model. Similarly, and drawing on the work of Pigott (1982), their argument was that American students' experiences of games teaching separated them from the "contextual nature of the skill and games teaching becomes a series of drills conforming to textbook techniques" (p. 8).

The tactical games approach is, in many ways, a simplification of teaching games for understanding. Game form remains at the centre of Griffin et al.'s (1997) model. It is supported by ideas of modification, representation, exaggeration and conditioning in an effort to encourage tactical thinking. Equally, tactical awareness and skill execution are included (and in the same hierarchical order) but that is where the model ends its mirroring of teaching games for understanding.

The predominant *sayings* expounded in Griffin et al.'s (1997) model are related to students' thinking and problem solving about and around developmentally appropriate games. As shown in Table 3.2, the learning aspirations of the tactical games approach model include students: (a) considering tactical solutions to problems presented in lessons, (b) practicing skills encountered in developmentally appropriate games, (c) linking games and skills through teacher questioning, and (d) applying practiced skills and increasing tactical understanding in developmentally appropriate games.

In arguing for a need for the tactical games approach model, Griffin et al. (1997) positioned games teaching, this time in the USA, as being predominately about the techniques and skills of games rather than their in-game use in response to tactical understanding. In short, they did not consider the *sayings* and *doings* of games teaching to be fit for purpose. Unlike Bunker and Thorpe (1986), however, they avoided the broader *relatings* surrounding physical education and focused, instead, on a broader definition of game performance that included "decision making, supporting, marking or guarding, covering teammates, adjusting position as game play unfolds, ensuring adequate court or field coverage by a base position" (Griffin et al., 1997, p. 12).

Our aim in this section is not to consider all GCAs. In retrospectively determining the practice architectures of teaching games for understanding and tactical games we are seeking to show what practice, considered as a main idea, critical elements, learning aspirations and pedagogy look like. We imagine that other GCAs would have different practice architectures with games sense's main idea, as an example, being development of "thinking players" (Pill & SeeSee, In Press). Our purpose is not to map every model. Instead it is to create a sustainable and understandable approach to MbP that might include GCAs.

Cooperative learning

Unlike the other pedagogical models explored in this book, the origins of cooperative learning lie outside physical education. It could be argued, however, that from that external vantage point the idea of cooperative learning as a pedagogical model makes little or no sense. Accordingly, it is not our aim to explore the *sayings*, *doings* and *relatings* of cooperative learning *per se*, but to try to track its beginnings and subsequent development as a pedagogical model in physical education. We do this by exploring two practitioner-orientated books on the subject and articulating what we see as their practice architectures. We begin with Terry Orlick's (1978) *The cooperative sports & games book* and conclude by exploring Ben Dyson and Ashley Casey's (2016) text *Cooperative learning in physical education and physical activity.*

Cooperative sports and games

As the factory has come to be a model for the organization of so much of Western life, so too have children's games been industrialized. The emphasis on production, machine orientation, and overspecialization has become as widespread in games as in industry. Games themselves have become rigid, judgemental, highly organised, and excessively goal-orientated. There is no freedom from the pressure of evaluation and the psychological distress of disapproval. In the end, the focus on squeezing the most out of every individual leaves no room for plain old fun.

(Orlick, 1978, p. 5)

In an argument similar to Lawson's (2009) criticism of the industrial age school, Orlick argued for cooperation as a counter-narrative to the performative *doings* inherent in traditional school physical education. He believed that the constant exposure of children to what he describes as "irrational competition" (p. 5) resulted in an unhealthy understanding of cooperation in which there is one winner and many losers.

In arguing for cooperation over competition, Orlick (1978, p. 3) asked, "have you ever seen the fun torn from a child's game? Have you ever seen children left out or put out by games, rejected, intentionally hurt, and wondered why?" The fact that many of us have witnessed or read about such outcomes, speaks volumes about both the *sayings* and *doings* of physical education that Orlick saw. In contrast to experiences where children are left on the outside looking in, Orlick advocated for games experiences that "provide beautiful occasions for challenge, stimulation, self-evaluation, success and sheer fun" (p. 4). Furthermore, he argued that while experiences such as these were once commonplace in the games of diverse cultures around the world, they are almost absent from North American culture in the 1970s (and, we would add, from British, Australasian and European cultures to name a few examples).

Competitive games, at least from Orlick's perspective, have conditioned the way young people *relate* to one another and society. He felt that

> they [children] have been so conditioned to the importance of winning that they can no longer play for fun, for enjoyment. They don't know how to help one another, to be sensitive to another's feelings, or to compete in a friendly, fun-filled way, even when they want to.
>
> (Orlick, 1978, p. 5)

In short, he felt that competitive games "taught" many kids unjustifiably "bad things" about themselves.

The predominantly anecdotal nature of Orlick's text makes it hard to determine the main idea, critical elements and learning aspirations of cooperative learning. Reading from an informed position, and taking a little poetic licence, we would argue that the main idea of *Cooperative sports and games* is not the games themselves but the experiences that lie behind them:

> The beauty of these games lies in part in their versatility and adaptability. For the most part, cooperative games require little or no equipment and virtually no outlay of cash. They can be used with a wide range of populations and in a variety of physical settings. Anyone can play them, almost anywhere. The "rules," or non-rules, of the specific games need not be strictly adhered to. You can work out your own specific details. You don't need a certain kind of ball to play with or a definite kind of field to play on. You don't even need to play in predetermined positions or for pre-set time periods. These things really don't matter. The important thing is the *concept behind the games*.
>
> (Orlick, 1978, p. 4, emphasis added)

Arguing for experiences in sport and games that helped students learn from their mistakes, without fear of adverse accountability for these mistakes, Orlick (1978) stated that there were four essential components (or critical elements) in a cooperative game:

Cooperation: "Related to communication, cohesiveness, trust, and the development of *positive social-interaction skills* . . . the players in the game must help one another by working as a unit – *each player being a necessary part of that unit* – and leaving no one out of the action" (Orlick, 1978, p. 7, emphasis added).

Acceptance: "Each child has a meaningful role to play within the game . . . each child is also at least *partially responsible for the* *accomplishment of a goal* or successful outcome of the game" (Orlick, 1978, p. 7, emphasis added).

Involvement: "directly related to a feeling of belonging, a sense of contribution, and satisfaction with the activity ... children want to be part of the action, not apart from it" (Orlick, 1978, p. 7).

Fun: "In cooperative ventures, the element of fun is enhanced as children are free to play with others, without fear of failure or rejection and without any need for destructiveness" (Orlick, 1978, p. 7).

These elements, whilst listed in Table 3.3 as critical elements, also provide us with an insight into the pedagogy of cooperative learning in physical

Table 3.3 The main idea, critical elements and learning aspirations of cooperative learning

Main Idea	Critical Elements	Learning Aspirations
"The important thing is the concept behind the game" (Orlick, 1978, p. 4). Learning with, by, from and for each other (Dyson & Casey, 2016)	Cooperation (including positive social-interaction skills) (Orlick, 1978) Promotive face-to-face interaction (Dyson & Casey, 2016)	Success is only achieved when work together and rely on one another (Dyson & Casey, 2016)
	Acceptance (partial responsibility for an accomplishment) (Orlick, 1978). Positive Interdependence (Dyson & Casey, 2016)	Students are answerable for their own learning (Dyson & Casey, 2016)
	Involvement (feeling of belonging and a sense of contribution) (Orlick, 1978). Individual Accountability (Dyson & Casey, 2016)	Students listen, share decision making, take responsibility, give and receive feedback, and lead, follow and encourage each other, (Dyson & Casey, 2016)
	Fun (playing without fear of failure or rejection) (Orlick, 1978)	Students take responsibility for own and others' learning (Dyson & Casey, 2016)
	Small group and interpersonal skills (Dyson & Casey, 2016) Group Processing (Dyson & Casey, 2016)	Students feel physically and emotionally safe (Dyson & Casey, 2016)

education. It is clear to see how these elements could influence the curriculum, teaching, learning and assessment found in a cooperative learning unit. Teachers, for example, would plan, teach and assess not just skills and techniques but students' cooperation, acceptance, involvement and their ability to engender fun for themselves and others.

Cooperative learning in physical education and physical activity

Writing nearly four decades later, Dyson and Casey (2016) had the luxury of drawing on nearly 40 years of research into cooperative learning in physical education. The main idea at the heart of their exploration of the model was that students learn with, by, from and for each other, i.e. students act in the belief that their goals can only be achieved if they work collectively and promote each other's efforts. (see Table 3.3 for more information). Fundamentally, Dyson and Casey held that cooperative learning could convey a version of physical education in which learning "occur[s] in classrooms which include each and every child" (p. 7). Whilst this is a well-rehearsed argument, Dyson and Casey (2016) differ from Orlick inasmuch as they wield the weight of subject-specific research in support of their arguments. Consequently, we learn more about the specific *sayings*, *doings* and *relatings* of cooperative learning in physical education.

Drawing on the first review of literature of cooperative learning in physical education (see Casey & Goodyear, 2015), Dyson and Casey directed readers beyond the expected motor and tactical outcomes of physical education and towards cognitive, social and affective learning. Furthermore, they highlighted other achievements attributable to cooperative learning:

> Research on cooperative learning in physical education has reported the improvement of interpersonal and social skills with a positive and supportive learning environment . . . helped develop students' social skills and attitudes towards group work . . . groups not only developed motor skills but also found empathy with and to other students, which in turn decreased their disruptive behaviours.
>
> (Dyson & Casey, 2016, pp. 17–18)

Dyson and Casey drew on the now familiar argument that the popular *doings* of multi-activity, sport technique-based physical education serve to teach most young people that they cannot do what is being asked of them. Equally, it teaches them that even their best efforts will seldom if ever be enough to overcome even the most half-hearted efforts of their most able peers. Cooperative learning, in contrast, challenges students to learn that when others develop and progress those gains are attributable to the group, and vice versa. The pedagogy of the model seeks to take value away from the individual and bestow it on the group. Accordingly, "success is defined in terms of team or group achievement and not individual prowess, and it (i.e. success) can only be achieved when everyone works together for a shared purpose" (Dyson & Casey, 2016, p. 8).

From a social-political perspective, the *relatings* of cooperative learning in physical education referred to by Dyson and Casey draw on global arguments for support. For example, they used the Organisation for Economic Cooperation and Development's (2013) report on *Innovative Learning Environments* to help them position cooperative learning as one of six pedagogies best suited to create the student-centred learning environment needed for the 21st Century. Contrariwise, Dyson and Casey discredit the common argument that physical education is replete with examples of teamwork and, as such, is already an inherently cooperative school subject. Putting children is groups/teams is not equivalent to using cooperative learning, nor is learning to cooperate a spontaneous outcome of playing team sports. Team games do not, in and of themselves, teach cooperation and teamwork (Hellison & Wright, 2003). The development of such things is a conscious part of the pedagogical process and, as such, needs to be planned for and prioritised. As such, and in addition to expected psychomotor, cognitive, social and affective developments, students learn to help, assist, support, encourage and praise their group mates in their efforts. Furthermore, they get to know and trust one another, to accept and support each other, improve their communication, and learn how to resolve conflicts in constructive ways.

In conclusion, and as Table 3.3 indicates, the main idea, critical elements and learning aspirations of cooperative learning in physical education have been evolving over decades, as have the practice architectures of the model. However, whilst the language has changed and the sources of support have become increasingly subject centred, the overall messages are similar: the game/skill is less important than the group (and the individuals therein), and we need to learn how to be cooperative and this requires a plethora of skills and a change in attitude.

Teaching personal and social responsibility

Teaching personal and social responsibility was developed by practitioner-researcher Don Hellison. In his earliest work, Hellison described his approach as humanistic physical education (Hellison, 1973). Kirk (2020) has argued that this approach was fundamentally concerned with social justice and could be regarded as a form of critical pedagogy, though Hellison never used this term. In his 1995 book *Teaching personal and social responsibility through physical activity*, Hellison argued that the model was primarily concerned with developing the life skills of alienated youth, "skills in and a disposition toward social competence, problem-solving, autonomy, and a sense of purpose and future" (1995, p. 8). The lack of such skills was, as he saw it, an intermediate social problem, sitting between root causes (such as poverty) and immediate causes (such as hunger). Education, using physical activity as the primary medium, was Hellison's contribution to social justice for alienated youth.

The language used (*sayings*) to describe and explain this work evolved over time as Hellison developed his program in collaboration with colleagues and students. In *Beyond bats and balls* (1978), Hellison described three goals for alienated youth: helping young people make their own self-body-world connection, developing a sense of community, and facilitating an active playful spirit. His concerns at this stage were centred on levels of awareness, from no awareness at all, to self-body awareness (Who am I?), to self-other awareness, to some kind of integration of these levels of awareness. He accepted his own understanding at this stage was "fuzzy."

In his later work, such as the approach reported in the 1995 book, Hellison's language evolved and the focus changed. Awareness was retained, as we will see, but his focus by the mid-1990s was on "responsibility." This word became a key semantic space for pedagogical work with teaching personal and social responsibility. Hellison retained from the *Beyond bats and balls* era the notion of levels. With responsibility as the focus, these ranged from a level zero irresponsibility, through participation and effort under supervision, self-direction, and caring about and helping others, to transference of these skills to life outside the gym. Another key term in this mature form of teaching personal and social responsibility was self-evaluation, the ability to reflect on and take responsibility for one's own behaviour.

In terms of *doings*, in the afterschool "clubs" that formed the seed ground for teaching personal and social responsibility, Hellison regularly offered three physical activities as the primary media for learning life skills. Basketball was included because young people wanted to play, volleyball because it offered a high level of cooperation and fitness activities because these could be individualised. Even though the focus was on social and emotional development of alienated and underserved youth, Hellison understood that developing physical competence was important for these young people, and so he took his role as teacher of these physical activities seriously in this respect. Just the same, he embedded a series of other *doings* into these physical activities, such as awareness talks, the five levels-in-action, decision-making, group meetings to deal with specific incidents arising in the classes, and reflection time. Within and supplementing these general strategies, Hellison provided detail of specific *doings* at each of the levels of responsibility. At all times he was concerned to give individuals a say in their involvement in a class and in the program, resulting in a highly customised and student-centred pedagogy.

In terms of *relatings*, these are clear from the language used to describe teaching personal and social responsibility. Respecting others' rights and feelings, willingness to participate with guidance from the teacher, caring about and helping others, and self-direction each provide explicit direction on the kinds of *relatings* central to the model. Hellison argued that physical activity settings are well-suited to personal and social development because "they are very emotional, interactive and, for some kids, attractive . . . kids 'show more of themselves' in physical activity settings" (1995, p. 1). He suggested too that, even though this is a highly individualised and student-centred pedagogy, the relationships the teacher establishes are crucially important. These, he argued, must embody the levels of responsibility. He wrote about the challenges of doing this. Building and sustaining such respectful, caring and facilitative relationships is not easy. He noted differences between himself and his students in age, social class, gender and education. Despite these barriers, he saw caring as fundamentally important, as was being genuine and honest, but also resilient and persistent.

The practice architectures of teaching personal and social responsibility have continued to develop as a pedagogical model in its own right, and also within the context of the Positive Youth Development (PYD) movement. In terms of *sayings*, Holt, Tink, Mandigo, and Fox (2008) note that PYD starts from a strengths-based concept of development rather than one of deficit-reduction. The term "social and emotional learning" is regularly applied to this work (Gordon, Jacobs, & Wright, 2016). Additional terminology includes self-awareness, self-management, social awareness and relationship skills, while most of the core concepts Hellison developed remain in use, such as respecting the rights and feelings of others, effort and teamwork, goal-setting and leadership (Fraser-Thomas, Côté, & Deakin, 2005; Mandigo, Corlett, & Anderson, 2008). The term "atmosphere" was introduced by Ward and Parker (2013). Drawing on Self-Determination Theory, they found that a positive atmosphere in the programme they studied was evident in relatedness among youth and between youth and adults, where people could be counted on, where there was a relaxed atmosphere, and a desire to learn. The actual activities of the program tend to resemble closely those used by Hellison, as do the relationships. A particular focus of this

PYD work has been on Hellison's aspiration that the life skills learned in these programs transfer to other areas of life (Walsh, Ozaeta, & Wright, 2010; Gordon et al., 2016).

Within the context of these distinctive practice architectures of teaching personal and social responsibility, and as you will see in Table 3.4, we can begin to discern the internal structure of a pedagogical model. The main idea could be stated as "learning life skills concerned with personal and social responsibility." The critical elements would appear to include, at the very least: forms of physical activity; embedded levels of

Table 3.4 The main idea, critical elements and learning aspirations of teaching personal and social responsibility

Main Idea	Critical Elements	Learning Aspirations
Developing the life skills of alienated youth (Hellison, 1995).	Awareness talks (Hellison, 1995). Activities aimed at facilitating self and collective awareness	Helping young people make their own self-body-world connection (Hellison, 1978)
Learning life skills concerned with personal and social responsibility		Developing a sense of community (Hellison, 1978)
	The five levels-in-action (Hellison, 1995). Embedded levels of responsibility in action	Facilitating an active playful spirit (Hellison, 1978)
		Respecting others' rights and feelings (Hellison, 1995).
		Respect for others
	Reflection time (Hellison, 1995). Decision-making (Hellison, 1995) Reflection and decision-making	Willingness to participate with guidance from the teacher (Hellison, 1995).
		Participation and effort
	Group meetings to deal with specific incidents arising in the classes (Hellison, 1995). Relationships of respect, care and trust	Caring about and helping others (Hellison, 1995) Self-direction (Hellison, 1995) Hellison's five levels
	Forms of physical activity	Transference of these skills to everyday life outside the gym

responsibility in action; activities aimed at facilitating self and collective awareness; reflection and decision-making; and relationships of respect, care and trust. The learning aspirations are stated at Hellison's five levels of respect for others, participation and effort, self-directing, caring and helping and, ultimately, the transference of these skills to everyday life outside the gym.

Activist approaches

Since the late 1990s Kim Oliver has pioneered an activist approach to working with adolescent girls in physical education. Oliver and Kirk (2015) brought together lessons learned from this work to create a prototype pedagogical model. An activist approach rests on three assumptions. The first is that knowledge is produced in collaboration and action between teachers and girls, and between girls themselves. The second is that while understanding the nature of girls' experiences of multi-activity sport, technique-based physical education is necessary, it is not sufficient to change that experience, and so activists also focus on "what might be" through a pedagogy of possibility. The third is that social transformation, including disruption of the dominant gender order, starts at the micro level in localised contexts.

Informed by these assumptions, the main idea of the activist approach is girls learning to value the physically active life, a concept borrowed from Siedentop (1996). Although in their original formulation of the model Oliver and Kirk (2015) did not explicitly critique the New Public Health appropriation of this health-related notion as a form of risk-management, Kirk's (2020) more recent account has located this main idea within a salutogenic theory of health promotion. As such, becoming disposed to being physically active daily is viewed as an important "generalised resistance resource" (Antonovsky, 1996) for keeping healthy rather than reducing the risk of illness.

The four critical elements of the model come directly from Oliver's activist work with girls and their teachers. These are student-centred pedagogy, pedagogies of embodiment, inquiry-based education centred-*in*-action, and teachers and other adults listening to respond over time. Aspirations for girls' learning are that they become able to name, critique, negotiate and where possible transform barriers to their physical activity engagement, enjoyment and learning.

Oliver has, through work with various collaborations, continued to field-test this pedagogical model both in school physical education (e.g. Lamb, Oliver, & Kirk, 2018) and in physical education teacher education

(Oliver et al., 2018). Other have also taken up her activist approach, in the USA (Fisette, 2013), in Ireland (Enright & O'Sullivan, 2012) and Norway (Walseth, Engebretsen, & Elvebakk, 2018), although none of this work has been with the activist pedagogical model specifically.

One program of research that has sought to further elaborate the activist pedagogical model is Carla Luguetti's work in a community soccer program for socially vulnerable youth in Brazil (e.g. Luguetti, Oliver, Kirk, & Dantas, 2017). The main idea of this elaborated model was "co-constructing empowering possibilities through sport for youth from socially vulnerable backgrounds." Two critical elements from Oliver and Kirk's model were incorporated, student-centred pedagogy and inquiry-based education centred-*in*-action. Three new critical elements were an ethic of care, a community of sport, and attentiveness to community. New learning aspirations were becoming responsible and committed, communicating with others, valuing each other's knowledge, and learning from mistakes.

The practice architectures of this pedagogical model for working with girls and with socially vulnerable youth (see Table 3.5) bring together a

Table 3.5 The main idea, critical elements and learning aspirations of an activist approach to working with girls in physical education

Main Idea	Critical Elements	Learning Aspirations
Girls learning to value the physically active life (Oliver & Kirk, 2015)	Student-centred pedagogy (Lamb et al., 2018)	Teachers and pupils co-constructing the curriculum Name, critique, negotiate and change barriers to participation in physical activity
	Pedagogies of embodiment (Kirk et al., 2018)	Teachers and pupils co-constructing the environment to create safe spaces for learning Confidence, perseverance and resilience while engaging in the movement culture
	Inquiry-based education centred in action (Oliver et al., 2013)	Developing critical literacy skills for analysing and deconstructing damaging myths and ideologies Research skills to generate, analyse and collate information relating to barriers to participation
	Listening and responding over time	Learning to trust, respect and communicate with others Teachers authorise students' voices

number of *sayings*, such as valuing, student-centredness, embodiment, care, community, inquiry and action, and listening to respond. In terms of *doings*, both versions of the model involve what Oliver calls "Building the Foundation" (Oliver et al., 2013), an explicit and intentional process of young people learning to work together to co-construct their physical education and soccer learning experiences, involving setting and agreeing guidelines on relationships, cooperation, respect for others, commitment and responsibility. Indeed, these *doings* closely converge with the *relatings*, where teachers and coaches "authorise" the voices of young people and share responsibility for the construction and conduct of the learning program with them. Choice for the young people is then another important *doing*, and this relates to sampling and selecting physical activities for girls and how training and match play were conducted for the socially vulnerable young people.

Conclusion

Our purpose in this chapter has been to respond to the question of whether various approaches to physical education might be described as pedagogical models, as we have defined this term in the preceding two chapters, even though the originators may not have done so. In each case, we think it is possible to recast these approaches as pedagogical models that have a main idea, critical elements and learning aspirations, and to identify the alignment of curriculum, teaching and assessment in order to realise specific and distinctive learning aspirations.

By recasting these approaches as pedagogical models, we argue that we gain much more than we lose. As pedagogical models, with recognisable and distinctive practice architectures of *sayings*, *doings* and *relatings*, the particular educational benefits to be derived for young people from each model become clearer. Thus, their deployment in school programs can be more purposeful and better informed than traditional approaches. Moreover, with some common features such as main ideas, critical elements and learning aspirations, we have a meta-language with which to create a discourse about pedagogy in physical education that arguably we currently lack. This uniformity of key structural features also facilitates judgements about the fidelity of practice to the model, where the pedagogical model is a design specification for practice rather than a prescription. This is a key issue in managing the tension between agency external and internal to the school.

We suggest that if these approaches to physical education are reconceptualised and redeveloped as pedagogical models, we have the heartbeat of

MbP. However, if these and other models are to construct and constitute MbP in physical education, we must move beyond the writings of the originators, since this foundational work was done in the quite different cultural, political and economic times of the 1970s, 1980s and 1990s. For all the approaches described here, there have been important programs of empirical research upon which to draw in this process of recasting them as pedagogical models. In the next chapter, we take a further step in this process to explore the wider literature on models-based approaches in order to show how teacher-researchers, and teachers working with researchers, provide insights into the further elaboration of some of these approaches as pedagogical models.

References

Antonovsky, A. (1996). The salutogenic model as a theory to guide health promotion. *Health Promotion International, 11*(1), 11–18.

Bunker, D., & Thorpe, R. (1982). A model for teaching games in secondary school. *Bulletin of Physical Education, 10,* 9–16.

Bunker, D., & Thorpe, R. (1986). The curriculum model. In R. Thorpe, D. Bunker, & L. Almond (Eds.), *Rethinking games teaching* (pp. 7–10). Loughborough: University of Technology.

Caillois, R. (1961). *Man, play, and games.* London: Thames and Hudson.

Casey, A., & Goodyear, V. A. (2015). Can cooperative learning achieve the four learning outcomes of physical education? A review of literature. *Quest, 67*(1), 56–72.

Curtner-Smith, M. D., Todorovich, J. R., Lacon, S. A., & Kerr, I. A. (1999). Teachers' rules, routines, and expectations prior to and following the implementation of the national curriculum for physical education. *European Journal of Physical Education, 4*(1), 17–30.

Dyson, B., & Casey, A. (2016). *Cooperative learning in physical education and physical activity: A practical introduction.* London: Routledge.

Enright, E., & O'Sullivan, M. (2012). Physical education "in all sorts of corners". *Research Quarterly for Exercise and Sport, 83*(2), 255–267.

Fisette, J. L. (2013). "Are you listening?": Adolescent girls voice how they negotiate self-identified barriers to their success and survival in physical education. *Physical Education and Sport Pedagogy, 18*(2), 184–203.

Fraser-Thomas, J. L., Côté, J., & Deakin, D. (2005). Youth sport programs: An avenue to foster positive youth development. *Physical Education and Sport Pedagogy, 10*(1), 1.

Gordon, B., Jacobs, J. M., & Wright, P. M. (2016). Social and emotional learning through a teaching personal and social responsibility based after-school program for disengaged middle-school boys. *Journal of Teaching in Physical Education, 35*(4), 358–369.

Grehaigne, J. F. (1989). *Football de mouvement: Vers une approche systémique du jeu* [*Soccer in movement: Towards a systemic approach of the game*] (Unpublished doctoral dissertation). Université de Bourgogne, Dijon, France.

Grehaigne, J. F., Richard, J. F., & Griffin, L. L. (2005). *Teaching and learning team sports and games*. London: Routledge.

Griffin, L. L., Mitchell, S. A., & Oslin, J. L. (1997). *Teaching sport concepts and skills: A tactical games approach*. Champaign, IL: Human Kinetics.

Hellison, D. (1973). *Humanistic physical education*. Englewood Cliffs, NJ: Prentice-Hall.

Hellison, D. (1978). *Beyond balls and bats: Alienated (and other) youth in the gym*. Washington, DC: American Alliance for Health, Physical Education, Recreation, and Dance.

Hellison, D. (1995). *Teaching responsibility through physical activity*. Champaign, IL: Human Kinetics.

Hellison, D., & Wright, P. (2003). Retention in an urban extended day program: A process-based assessment. *Journal of Teaching in Physical Education, 22,* 369–381.

Holt, N. L., Tink, L. N., Mandigo, J. L., & Fox, K. R. (2008). Do youth learn life skills through their involvement in high school sport? A case study. *Canadian Journal of Education/Revue canadienne de l'éducation, 31*(2), 281–304.

Kemmis, S. (2019). *A practice sensibility: An invitation to the theory of practice architectures*. Singapore: Springer.

Kirk, D. (2010). *Physical education futures*. London: Routledge.

Kirk, D. (2020). *Precarity, critical pedagogy and physical education*. London: Routledge.

Kirk, D., Lamb, C. A., Oliver, K. L., Ewing-Day, R., Fleming, C., Loch, A., & Smedley, V. (2018). Balancing prescription with teacher and pupil agency: Spaces for manoeuvre within a pedagogical model for working with adolescent girls. *The Curriculum Journal, 29*(2), 219–237.

Lamb, C. A., Oliver, K. L., & Kirk, D. (2018). "Go for it girl": Adolescent girls' responses to the implementation of an activist approach in a core physical education programme. *Sport, Education and Society, 23*(8), 799–811.

Lawson, H. L. (2009). Paradigms, exemplars and social change. *Sport, Education and Society, 14*(1), 97–119.

Luguetti, C., Oliver, K. L., Kirk, D., & Dantas, L. (2017). Exploring an activist approach of working with boys from socially vulnerable backgrounds in a sport context. *Sport, Education and Society, 22*(4), 493–510.

Mandigo, J. L., Corlett, J., & Anderson, A. (2008). Using quality physical education to promote positive youth development in a developing nation: Striving for peace education. In N. Holt & R. Bailey (Eds.), *Positive youth development* (pp. 109–120). New York: Taylor & Francis.

Oliver, K. L., & Kirk, D. (2015). *Girls, gender and physical education: An activist approach*. New York: Routledge.

64   *Architectures of pedagogical models*

Oliver, K. L., Luguetti, C., Aranda, R., Nuñez Enriquez, O., & Rodriguez, A. A. (2018). "Where do I go from here?": Learning to become activist teachers through a community of practice. *Physical Education and Sport Pedagogy*, *23*(2), 150–165.

Oliver, K. L., Oesterreich, H. A., Aranda, R., Archeleta, J., Blazera, C., de la Cruza, K., . . . Robinson, R. (2013). "The sweetness of struggle": Innovation in physical education teacher training through student-centered inquiry as curriculum in a physical education methods course. *Physical Education and Sport Pedagogy*, *20*(1), 97–115.

Organisation for Economic Cooperation and Development (OECD). (2013). *Innovative learning environments*. Paris: OECD. Retrieved June 14, 2020, from www.oecd-ilibrary.org/education/innovative-learning-environments/executive-summary_9789264203488-2-en

Orlick, T. (1978). *The cooperative sports & games book: Challenge without competition*. New York: Pantheon Books.

Pigott, B. (1982). A psychological basis for new trends in games teaching. *Bulletin of Physical Education*, *18*(1), 17–22.

Pill, S., & SeeSee, B. (In Press). The game sense approach as play with purpose. In S. Pill (Ed.), *Perspectives on game-based coaching*. London: Routledge.

Schatzki, T. R. (2002). *The site of the social: A philosophical account of the constitution of social life and change*. University Park, PA: University of Pennsylvania Press.

Siedentop, D. (1982). *Movement and sport education: Current reflections and future images*. Paper presented at the Commonwealth and International Conference on Sport, Physical Education, Recreation, and Dance, Brisbane, Australia.

Siedentop, D. (1994). *Sport education: Quality PE through positive sport experiences*. Champaign, IL: Human Kinetics.

Siedentop, D. (1996). Valuing the physically active life: Contemporary and future directions. *Quest*, *48*(3), 266–274.

Siedentop, D. (2002). Sport education: A retrospective. *Journal of Teaching in Physical Education*, *21*, 409–418.

Siedentop, D., Hastie, P. A., & van der Mars, H. (2004). *Complete guide to sport education*. Champaign, IL: Human Kinetics.

Siedentop, D., Mand, C., & Taggart, A. (1986). *Physical education: Teaching and curriculum strategies for grades 5–12*. Mountain View, CA: Mayfield Publishing Company.

Thorpe, R., & Bunker, D. (1986). Landmarks on our way to "teaching for understanding". In R. Thorpe, D. Bunker, & L. Almond (Eds.), *Rethinking games teaching* (pp. 5–6). Loughborough: University of Technology.

Thorpe, R., Bunker, D., & Almond, L. (1986). *Rethinking games teaching*. Loughborough: University of Technology.

Walseth, K., Engebretsen, B., & Elvebakk, L. (2018). Meaningful experiences in PE for all students: An activist research approach. *Physical Education and Sport Pedagogy*, *23*(3), 235–249.

Walsh, D., Ozaeta, J., & Wright, P. (2010). Transference of responsibility model goals to the school environment: Exploring the impact of a coaching club program. *Physical Education and Sport Pedagogy, 15*(1), 15–28.

Ward, S., & Parker, M. (2013). The voice of youth: Atmosphere in positive youth development program. *Physical Education and Sport Pedagogy, 18*(5), 534–548.

Whitehead, N. J., & Hendry, L. B. (1976). *Teaching physical education in England, description and analysis*. London: Lepus Books.

4 A meso practice architectures perspective of four pedagogical models

Introduction

In Chapter 2, we engaged in what Lund and Tannehill (2005, p. 310) call "backward design" to identify three common features of pedagogical models i.e. the main idea, the critical elements and the learning aspirations. In Chapter 3 we adopted a macro perspective and retrospectively fitted these features and practice architectures (the *sayings*, *doings* and *relatings*) to a number of well-known pedagogical models. In this chapter we take this process a step further and apply these ideas and practice architectures to six reviews of literature on four different pedagogical models. Our aim in doing this is to understand, from a meso perspective, the manner in and degree to which the use of different pedagogical models has remained true to the aspirations of model-makers and advocates. We position these overviews of research as both synopses of or proxies for what people have done with pedagogical models in schools, and out-of-school and sport settings, and as examples of practice architectures in play. It is beyond the scope of this chapter – this book perhaps – to repeat this process across every model and every review. Consequently, the examples we provide here are intended as illustrations of what might be possible with other pedagogical models.

To position this synopsis of practice, we have taken a meso perspective and examined reviews of literature of four pedagogical models (sport education [Hastie, de Ojeda, & Calderón, 2011; Hastie & Wallhead, 2016], game-centred approaches [Harvey & Jarrett, 2014] cooperative learning [Casey & Goodyear, 2015] and teaching personal and social responsibility [Baptista et al., 2020; Richards & Shiver, Ahead of Print]). We do this with two main purposes: (1) to explore the plausibility and usefulness of our proposed framework for pedagogical models, and (2) to understand what these proxies for practice tell us about the potential for enactment of MbP. Our foci for this critique are the three components of practice architectures:

sayings, doings and *relatings* (see Chapter 2 for a fuller explanation). In particular, we have sought to better understand the extent to which authors have made explicit the main idea, critical elements and learning aspirations of their respective model or whether these have remained as implicit facets (or givens) in their work. Finally, we explore the curriculum, teaching, learning and assessment (i.e. pedagogy) reported in each review and sought to understand whether the retrospective application of our key ideas to published reviews of literature of specific models allows us to better understand the use of individual pedagogical models and the possibility of MbP.

We conclude the chapter by suggesting that review authors have replaced or overlooked important facets of the conceptual frameworks developed by model-makers in their efforts to report on the successes and areas for future research in their respective models. We see this as a fracturing of the macro ideas of model-makers and advocates, even though many of these authors occupy both spaces. We are also wary of the use of old justifications for physical education in the defence and support of new practice (i.e. the traditional "big 5" aims of PE [Alexander & Luckman, 2001, p. 254]). In both these cases we lose track of some of what we see as the signature practice architectures of these models. Consequently, and in keeping with a game like Telephone, what people do in practice appears to differ from what was originally intended. This further highlights the need to acknowledge that transformation in the process of implementation is inevitable. Consequently, local adaptations built on the aspirations, not the certainty, of any given pedagogical model are important when adopting MbP.

Sport education

In their *review of research on Sport Education: 2004 to present*, Hastie et al. (2011) followed the format of an earlier review by Wallhead and O'Sullivan (2005) in comparing the recent literature of the model in order to:

> (1) present an update on the research since 2005; (2) identify any new trends in the research since the original review; and (3) describe the extent to which the limitations and future directions of Wallhead and O'Sullivan's paper had been addressed.
>
> (p. 104)

Drawing on a critical mass of literature in sport education, Hastie et al. (2011) highlight the increasing strength of the *sayings* of sport education and suggest that the model has currency in the language and ideas of physical education. Equally, by examining not only the findings of the 38 studies in their review, but also the geographical location of the season, grade levels used, sports studied, and methodologies used, Hastie and colleagues argue that the *sayings*, i.e. that sport education consists of seasons, affiliation, formal competition, culminating events, record keeping and festivity, have been established in a body of research that pre-dates their own. Put simply, sport education is not only extensively talked about but is also deeply prevalent in the *doings* of the scholarly field (and to a lesser extent the school-based practice) of physical education.

The *relatings* of sport education are articulated through "five common content standards (i.e. motor skill development, tactical knowledge and performance, fitness, social development and student attitudes and values)" (Hastie et al., 2011, p. 103). What Alexander and Luckman (2001, p. 254) refer to as "the traditional 'big 5' aims of PE." In demonstrating what sport education brings to a site that might wish to use the model, Hastie et al. (2011) show how sport education is capable of disrupting both practice traditions and practice landscapes. Using language such as moderate to vigorous physical activity (MVPA), development of skill, physical/social development, fair play and lower skilled, Hastie et al. (2011) deploy arguments for sport education pre-2004 in the spaces in which the *sayings*, *doings* and *relatings* of physical education exist.

In adding the post-2004 element of their review to the wider literature they extend the existing arguments for sport education to included additional sites of practice, enhanced student motivation, and the experiences of pre-service and in-service teachers learning to teach sport education. Whilst the review is replete with examples of the learning aspirations and pedagogy (i.e. teaching, learning, curriculum and assessment) of sport education, it leaves consideration of the main idea and learning aspirations of the model until the conclusion. In closing Hastie et al. (2011, p. 129) assert that the main learning aspiration of sport education is "to educate students to be players in the fullest sense and to help them develop as competent, literate and enthusiastic sportspersons" (Siedentop, 1994, p. 5). Going further they suggest that:

> If an executive summary of the literature concerning those goals were to be made, it could be suggested that evidence for competency is "burgeoning and developing", support for literacy is "emerging", and that enthusiastic responses by students have been "significantly substantiated".
>
> (Hastie et al., 2011, p. 129)

Consequently, while sport education is presented as a model with both a rich history and meaningful future in the practice architectures of physical education, the nuances of what such practice might look like are somewhat overlooked.

In Hastie and Wallhead's (2016) consideration of MbP in physical education, *the case for sport education* is made quite differently. They open the paper with a clear statement of belief, that "when taught with the full set of benchmarks [or critical elements for the purposes of this book] of the model, sport education seasons can achieve Siedentop's (1994) original short-term objectives" (Hastie & Wallhead, 2016, p. 390). This statement is both an acknowledgement of the main idea and learning aspirations of sport education (which they quickly state as "student competence, literacy and enthusiastic participation" (p. 390)) and the intersubjective *sayings* of sport education. In each sub-section of the paper, which track the main idea and learning aspirations of competence, literacy and enthusiasm from the early years in the 1990s, through the new millennium, and into the recent past of 2010 to 2016, Hastie and Wallhead (2016) explore the *sayings*, *doings* and *relatings* of sport education.

In their road-mapping of sport education, Hastie and Wallhead repeatedly present the *sayings* of the model as recognisable and desirable constructs i.e. skill development, game-based learning and persisting teams in the 1990s; skill, knowledge and game performance in the 2000s; and organisation, motivation and health in the 2010s and beyond. This laying-down of foundations and expectations for sport education is followed by a detailed consideration of the *doings* that have been reported over the decades and what can be expected in the near future. They argue, for example, that sport education has moved from a situation where student coaches struggled with the higher order responsibility of their roles, to one where student-coach acumen is being developed over several seasons and is supported by examples from a cross-pollination of teacher and coach education.

The maturity of sport education is further exemplified in Hastie and Wallhead's (2016) exploration of the developing *relatings* of the model. Given the remarkable endurance of direct instruction, it is unsurprising to see these authors make a case for sport education because it is deemed better than direct instruction at improving students of all skill levels. Similarly, and at a time when student voice and democracy are of increasing importance (Dyson, 2006), it is unsurprising that the authors highlight sport education's potential to enhance the relationships and feelings of status that exist amongst students in every classroom. While motivation is mentioned, in our opinion, as one of the *doings* of sport education, it is also used as a justification for enhanced *relatings* attributable to use of this pedagogical model. Therefore, and from a *relatings* perspective, sport education is shown to enhance the enthusiasm of lower achieving and amotivated students, can help with the health development of young people, and (drawing on the work of Oslin [2002] cited in Hastie and Wallhead [2016, p. 397]) provide "bridging activities that link what students learn in Sport Education to the larger sport and physical activity cultures of the community which may serve to enhance visibility as well as transferability."

In general, therefore, it seems that the *sayings*, *doings* and *relatings* of sport education, and to a lesser extent the model's main idea, critical elements, learning aspirations and pedagogy, can be mapped from these two different reviews of the literature. Throughout our reading of this work it is clear that strong justifications for the model are being made in the semantic, physical and social spaces of schools and pedagogies. Nonetheless, support for sport education because it is better than multi-activity, sport technique-based physical education at achieving the traditional outcomes of the subject, is a concern. This is especially true given extensive criticism of these traditional outcomes by physical education scholars (Ennis, 2014; Kirk, 2010; Locke, 1992), if not the teaching profession more broadly (McMillan, 2017).

Game-centred approaches

Harvey and Jarrett (2014, p. 279) borrowed the term "game-centred approaches" (GCA) from a previous review by Oslin and Mitchell (2006) and argued that there are four prominent GCAs: "teaching games for understanding (TGfU; Bunker & Thorpe, 1982); play practice (PP; Launder, 2001); the tactical games models (TGM; Mitchell, Oslin, & Griffin, 2006); and game sense (GS; Light, 2004)." In a nearly identical vein to both Wallhead and O'Sullivan (2005) and Hastie et al. (2011), Harvey and Jarrett (2014, p. 279) organise their review around what they term the "5 big aims of PE", i.e. (1) motor skill development, (2) tactical knowledge and game performance, (3) fitness, (4) personal social development, and (5) students' attitudes and values.

Before returning to Harvey and Jarrett's paper, it is helpful to consider the practice architectures at play here. The positioning, firstly, of sport education (as mentioned earlier) and, latterly, GCAs as achievers of the "big 5" draws its justification from Alexander and Luckman's (2001) analysis of *Australian teachers' perceptions and uses of the sport education curriculum model*. In this paper, Alexander and Luckman (2001, p. 254) seem to arbitrarily position "motor skill" development, "fitness," "social development," "values and attitudes" and "knowledge and understanding" as the traditional "big 5" aims of PE. There is no empirical nor theoretical support for this claim in their paper and yet it has become a semantic bedrock (or *saying*) for the reviews of both sport education (Hastie et al., 2011; Hastie &

Wallhead, 2016; Wallhead & O'Sullivan, 2005) and GCAs (Harvey & Jarrett, 2014). While an argument might be retrospectively made to justify the "big 5," we need to recognise the *sayings* of a number of authors who argue for single model MbP. Such arguments are not impartial as they seek to position one model or approach on par with, or indeed ahead of, other instructional, curriculum or pedagogical approaches such as direct instruction (what we would see as multi-activity, sport technique-based physical education). While it is outside the scope of this chapter, it is important that we distance ourselves from the "big 5" discourse at this point and look instead at the alignment of curriculum, teaching, learning and assessment in each model.

Returning to the review paper, it is conceivable, given the number of versions of the game-centred approach covered in their review, that Harvey and Jarrett (2014) consciously chose to make no discernible attempt to articulate the main idea of either GCAs generally, or the four prominent models specifically. In not doing so, however, they assume that the reader understands the substantive nature of each model and the key similarities and differences. This assumption is perhaps doubly or even triply true when neither critical elements nor learning aspirations are discussed. Nonetheless, Harvey and Jarrett (2014) make a series of strong arguments regarding the practice architectures of GCAs represented in the 44 papers that make up their review.

Following on from the "big 5" argument, the remaining *sayings* of GCAs relate predominantly to the places (which countries research is coming from) and/or context (schools or sport clubs), people (teachers, coaches and/or students) and perceived enhancements (to student engagement, tactical development, fun and inclusivity) associated with GCAs. In contrast, and as might be expected from such a review, GCAs *doings* revolve around what reportedly has been done in the physical spaces where they are used. These included "conceptual and instructional difficulties . . . pedagogical and time constraints" (Harvey & Jarrett, 2014, p. 289) and "teachers' and coaches' difficulties in both conceptual understanding of GCAs and in the implementation" (p. 290). What the authors did not do, however, was consider the ways in which, for example, questioning occurred, or modified games were developed and used. In short, the *doings* of GCS's were pedagogically rather than practically focused. Whilst lauding the impact of GCAs, Harvey and Jarrett (2014, p. 294) also lamented the lack of studies "with students with special educational needs or within disabled populations both in physical education and sport club contexts." They concluded that pre-service teachers, in-service teachers and coaches lacked "confidence in their ability to engage students with high-level questioning, conceptual and instructional difficulties, an entrenched mindset, perceived behavioural control, and ped-agogical and time constraints associated with planning and delivery" (Har-vey & Jarrett, 2014, p. 295). Given the constraints inherent in *doing* GCA it is important that researchers are more explicit in their articulation of the main idea, critical elements, learning aspirations and pedagogy of GCAs. Such vocalisation could help readers to better understand the very things that were barriers for previous users of GCAs.

The *relatings* of GCAs, i.e. the understanding of power, solidarity and social space, suggested that game play and sports are not singular concepts but are, instead, subject to cultural interpretation which, in turn, affect the experiences of participants. These interpretations include the traditional role of the coach and the teacher as dominant and in control. The power of existing practice suggests that GCAs are forces to compete with embedded expectations (a) that winning is more important than player development and understanding, and (b) involving players in decision-making will auto-matically compromise the authority of the coach. Such established *relatings* mean it is harder for GCAs to affect the existing practice architectures of games teaching and coaching.

Despite an underlying sense of frustration and ambiguity at the heart of the practice architectures of GCAs, the perceived "ability" of these approaches to address the "big 5," and an expansion of research into sport clubs and new global locations, is presented as a positive and GCAs are considered to have a place in the future of physical education. Our reading is somewhat different from that of Harvey and Jarrett (2014), Wallhead and O'Sullivan (2005) and Hastie et al. (2011) in their respective considerations of sport education) and raises a significant question: "Why would having a pedagogical model that replicates the outcomes of traditional physical education (i.e. the big 5) be something to celebrate?" This suggests slippage from the intentions of the model-makers and towards an accommodation of GCAs within multi-activity, sport technique-based physical education. Per-haps this analysis suggests that not all adaptations of pedagogical models to suit local contexts are desirable or defensible.

Cooperative learning

In their review of the cooperative learning literature, Casey and Goodyear (2015) asked *Can cooperative learning achieve the four learning outcomes of physical education?* Positioning this question in the title to their paper could be considered a ploy used to give credence to their argument. It could also be considered as an endorsement of tradition. The *sayings* of coopera-tive learning are further expounded in the paper's introduction where the authors legitimise both the physical, cognitive, social and affective domains in physical education and cooperative learning's "ability" to teach across these. Significantly, academic learning in cooperative learning in physical education was defined as learning in both the physical and cognitive domains and was shown to incorporate motor and tactical skill development in addition to social and affective learning. The *doings* of cooperative learning, in contrast, are limited by time (i.e. short units lasting between four and six weeks) which is, in turn, determined by timetables constrained by the dominance of the multi-activity curriculum. Such limitations illustrate our point that pedagogical models are frequently used within and not instead of multi-activity, sport technique-based physical education.

The *relatings* discussed in this review – as with the work of Orlick (1978) discussed in Chapter 2 – were borrowed from (and legitimised through) research into cooperative learning in mainstream education. Unlike both sport education and GCAs, cooperative learning has enjoyed widespread adaption and empirical research in numerous subject areas and across geographical contexts. It was this body of literature that Casey and Goodyear (2015) brought to bear in regard to *relatings* in physical education. In short, they argued that because cooperative learning worked elsewhere, and because it has a body of research which is the envy of other pedagogical models, this is an approach that has almost palpable power and solidarity in the social spaces of schools.

Despite the practice architectures noted above, and perhaps because of the comparatively few studies in physical education (when compared to the other reviews already considered in this chapter), Casey and Goodyear (2015) spent a considerable amount of time exploring the main idea of cooperative learning, i.e. learning with, by, from and for each other. In addition, they detail the critical elements (i.e. positive interdependence, individual accountability, group processing, promotive face-to-face interaction, and small group and interpersonal skills) and learning aspirations (e.g. "students are encourage to interact with each other and learn from the experiences they create largely by themselves" (Casey & Goodyear, 2015, p. 58)). Finally, details are provided, albeit less explicitly, about the teaching, learning, curriculum and assessment used previously in research into cooperative learning in physical education. This exploration of cooperative learning as a pedagogical model allows the reader to see a clearer relationship between the aspiration of model-makers and advocates than any of the other reviews.

Teaching personal and social responsibility

In the final couple weeks of writing this book two reviews of teaching personal and social responsibility literature came to our attention. The first, conducted by Baptista et al. (2020) systematically reviewed the literature around the model. In doing so the authors articulated the main idea (i.e. "that responsibility behaviours can be taught within the contexts of physical activity and can help youngsters adapting to transitions into adulthood" (p. 3)) and the critical elements (i.e. the five levels of responsibility). Beyond that, there were a number of assumptions made. Firstly, they anticipated a knowledgeable readership with regards to teaching personal and social responsibility and secondly, they did not articulate the *sayings*, *doing* and *relatings* in the way we have seen in other reviews of models. Finally, they focused on the approach to research and not the actualisation of teaching personal and social responsibility in different contexts and with different populations. As such, we were left to consider the operationalisation of the model in research and not the pedagogy or learning aspirations. Nonetheless, we did learn a little about improvements in behaviour, social outcomes, leadership, relationships, values, transference and the impact of teaching personal and social responsibility on staff.

The second review, Richards and Shiver's (Ahead of Print) *"What's worth doing?": A qualitative historical analysis of the TPSR model*, explores teaching personal and social responsibility through the back catalogue of Don Hellison's published works. Whilst this review differs from the others, inasmuch as it covers the lifework of the model's originator, it does highlight the development of the model from conceptual framework to pedagogical model and beyond into local curricula and back again (Jewett & Bain, 1985). As such, it provides an articulation of the practice architectures of teaching personal and social responsibility across nearly five decades.

Unlike Baptista et al. (2020), Harvey and Jarrett (2014) and Hastie et al. (2011), Richards and Shiver (Ahead of Print) make no assumptions of the reader's knowledge of teaching personal and social responsibility. Perhaps, this is a difference between a model like teaching personal and social responsibility which is "somewhere on the margins of kinesiology/physical education" (Hellison & Martinek, 2009, cited in Richards & Shiver, Ahead of Print, p. 1) and more established models like sport education and GCAs. Indeed, Richards and Shiver (Ahead of Print) articulate the main idea, critical elements, learning aspirations and pedagogy of teaching personal and social responsibility. For example, the critical elements are shown to be respect, participation, effort, self-direction and helping others, while the learning aspirations are "built around values associated with putting children first, empathy, care and compassion" (Richards & Shiver, Ahead of Print, p. 2). In fact, the review is replete with examples of these key aspects of a pedagogical model.

The *sayings* of teaching personal and social responsibility are centred on the aspiration to adopt a humanistic approach to youth development in physical education. In many respects this was "uncharted territory" (Richards & Shiver, Ahead of Print, p. 3) that "lacked support from the mainstream [physical education] community" (p. 3). While teaching personal and social responsibility saw the "delinquent kids" it did not position them as a problem but instead they were the focus of the model. This was a "departure from prevailing physical education practices which he [Hellison] believed to have adopted a narrow focus on physical development . . . [and] physical activity" Richards & Shiver, Ahead of Print, p. 3). More recently, and in keeping with a number of pedagogical models, teaching personal and social responsibility has moved closer to a social and emotional learning agenda.

For a long time physical education has been tagged with responsibility for disaffected kids outside of the classroom. These *doings* are taken up by teaching personal and social responsibility in this review. Richards and Shiver's (Ahead of Print) wrote about how "practitioners using the TPSR model seek to utilise young people's enjoyment of movement to explicitly practice and initiate discussions related to personally and socially responsible behaviour both inside and outside of the gym." They saw teaching personal and social responsibility as "an actionable approach to teaching" (p. 6) that helps practitioners move beyond viewing the model as a behaviour management strategy.

The teaching personal and social responsibility model has "grown" its *relatings* over time. They started with the need to connect with alienated and underserved youth (Richards & Shiver, Ahead of Print) in a subject that was more focused on physical activity than social and emotional learning. In many ways it was the antithesis of multi-activity, sport technique-based physical education, but consequently teaching personal and social responsibility has continued "to live on the margins of the field" (p. 8). This has meant that the model has been developed and redeveloped over time to meet the needs of all young people but especially those seen as the "delinquent kids." As such it could be positioned as the poster child for the process of reconceptualisation envisioned by Jewett and Bain (1985) and articulated by Casey (2016).

Conclusion

Despite the variance in detail provided in these reviews, we can begin to gain a sense of what the practice architectures of individual models might look like when they are used in schools and other learning contexts. We also get a sense of what is explicitly articulated and what, perhaps, is implicitly assumed. The different reviews considered in this chapter serve as proxies for what people have actually done at a meso level with single pedagogical models. Nonetheless, we are left to question if these authors, in reporting closely about what selected research has conveyed, are bringing to light a large-scale shift away from the nuances of model-makers aspirations in the studies they have reviewed. Alternatively, have their reinterpretations of other people's empirical studies introduced outdated notions (such as the "big 5") which only serve to supplant, or obscure important facets of the conceptual frameworks developed by the model-makers and advocates themselves? In doing the latter, there is a risk that we will lose track of what we see as the fundamentals (i.e. the main idea, the critical elements and the learning aspirations) of a pedagogical model and therefore ultimately of MbP. Consequently, and in keeping with a game like Telephone, what people actually do appears to differ from what was initially intended. This further highlights the need to consider local adaptions and the aspirations, not certainties, of any given pedagogical models. Furthermore, the fracturing of macro ideas and a reliance, a dependence even, on old justifications for new practice tempers the benchmarks seen by Metzler (2000) into the aspirations we envision for models. Conversely, however, an over-dilution of the main idea, the critical elements and the learning aspirations risks divesting a pedagogical model of its signature practice architectures and of denying users some sense of what the creators of the model regarded as its unique and essential features.

In the next chapter we take this analysis a step further, to the micro level of individual studies of selected pedagogical models. In this chapter, the discourse around the effective (or otherwise) implementation of four pedagogical models was mediated by the voices of the authors of the literature reviews we analysed. In the next chapter, a shift in focus to the micro level provides a closer view of the forces at work during the practice of pedagogical models in specific sites.

References

Alexander, K., & Luckman, J. (2001). Australian teachers' perceptions and uses of the sport education curriculum model. *European Physical Education Review*, 7(3), 243–267.

Baptista, C., Corte-Real, N., Regueiras, L., Seo, G., Hemphill, M., Pereira, A., . . . Fonseca, A. (2020). Teaching personal and social responsibility after school: A systematic review. *Cuadernos de Psicología del Deporte*, 20(2), 1–25.

Bunker, D., & Thorpe, R. (1982). A model for teaching games in secondary school. *Bulletin of Physical Education*, 10, 9–16.

Casey, A. (2016). Models-based practice. In C. D. Ennis (Ed.), *Routledge handbook of physical education pedagogies* (pp. 54–67). London: Routledge.

Casey, A., & Goodyear, V. A. (2015). Can cooperative learning achieve the four learning outcomes of physical education? A review of literature. *Quest, 67*(1), 56–72.

Dyson, B. (2006). Students' perspectives of physical education. In D. Kirk, D. MacDonald, & M. O'Sullivan (Eds.), *The handbook of physical education* (pp. 326–46). Thousand Oaks, CA: Sage.

Ennis, C. D. (2014). What goes around comes around . . . or does it? Disrupting the cycle of traditional, sport-based physical education. *Kinesiology Review, 3*, 63–70.

Harvey, S., & Jarrett, K. (2014). A review of the game-centred approaches to teaching and coaching literature since 2006. *Physical Education and Sport Pedagogy, 19*(3), 278–300.

Hastie, P. A., de Ojeda, D. M., & Calderón, A. (2011). A review of research on sport education: 2004 to the present. *Physical Education and Sport Pedagogy, 16*(2), 103–132.

Hastie, P. A., & Wallhead, T. (2016). Models-based practice in physical education: The case for sport education. *Journal of Teaching in Physical Education, 35*(4), 390–399.

Hellison, D., & Martinek, T. (2009). Living in the margins of our field. In L. D. Housner, M. W. Metzler, P. G. Schempp, & T. J. Templin (Eds.), *Historic traditions and future directions of research on teaching and teacher education in physical education* (pp. 267–270). Morgantown, WV: Fitness Information Technology.

Jewett, A. E., & Bain, L. L. (1985). *The curriculum process in physical education*. Dubuque, IA: Wm. C. Brown.

Kirk, D. (2010). *Physical education futures*. London: Routledge.

Launder, A. (2001). *Play practice: The games approach to teaching and coaching sports*. Adelaide: Human Kinetics.

Light, R. (2004). Coaches' experiences of game sense: Opportunities and challenges. *Physical Education and Sport Pedagogy, 9*(2), 115–131.

Locke, L. F. (1992). Changing secondary school physical education. *Quest, 44*(3), 361–372.

Lund, J., & Tannehill, D. (2005). *Standards-based physical education curriculum development*. Sudbury, MA: Jones & Bartlett Publishers.

McMillan, P. (2017). Understanding physical education teachers' day-to-day practice: Challenging the "unfair" picture. In M. Thorburn (Ed.), *Transformative learning and teaching in physical education* (pp. 159–175). London: Routledge.

Metzler, M. W. (2000). *Instructional models for physical education*. Needham Heights, MA: Allyn and Bacon.

Mitchell, S. A., Oslin, J. L., & Griffin, L. L. (2006). *Teaching sport concepts and skills: A tactical games approach* (2nd ed.). Champaign, IL: Human Kinetics.

Orlick, T. (1978). *The cooperative sports & games book: Challenge without competition*. New York: Pantheon Books.

Oslin, J. (2002). Sport education: Cautions, considerations, and celebrations. *Journal of Teaching in Physical Education, 21*, 419–426.

Oslin, J., & Mitchell, S. (2006). Game-centred approaches to teaching physical education. In D. Kirk, D. MacDonald, & M. O'Sullivan (Eds.), *The handbook of physical education* (pp. 627–651). London: Sage.

Richards, K. A. R., & Shiver, V. N. (Ahead of Print). "What's worth doing?": A qualitative historical analysis of the TPSR model. *Journal of Teaching in Physical Education.*

Siedentop, D. (1994). *Sport education: Quality PE through positive sport experiences.* Champaign, IL: Human Kinetics.

Wallhead, T., & O'Sullivan, M. (2005). Sport education: Physical education for the new millennium? *Physical Education and Sport Pedagogy, 10*(2), 181–210.

5 The implementation and reconfiguration of pedagogical models at the micro level

From articulation to actualisation

Introduction

Over the course of the book we have increasingly refined our focus on pedagogical models from the macro (Chapter 3), through the meso (Chapter 4) and now into the micro. Having engaged in what Lund and Tannehill (2005, p. 310) call "backward design" we have retrospectively fitted the features (i.e. the main ideas, critical elements, learning aspirations and pedagogy) and practice architectures (the *sayings*, *doings* and *relatings*) to (a) a number of pedagogical models (macro level) and (b) a number of reviews of literature on uses of pedagogical models (meso level). In this chapter we take a next step and apply these ideas to empirical research papers (micro level). Specifically, we apply our belief that each model serves as a design specification for local curriculum planning and explore the ways in which researchers have, or indeed have not, used or adapted the main idea, critical elements, learning aspirations and pedagogy of each model in their study.

The act of implementing a pedagogical model, at least in terms of how it is reported in the literature, is empirical. Consequently, *stories* of teachers' and students' engagements with pedagogical models are filtered through the lens of research, most particularly via practitioner and other participatory methodologies. Hence stories of changes to "practices, people's understandings of their practices, and the conditions under which they practice" (Kemmis, 2009, p. 464) provide us with a somewhat formal narrative of pedagogical model use. In some ways, this limits our broader understanding of pedagogical models (because the full extent of model use goes unreported) but, in other ways, this rigorous reporting of research findings is more fortuitous than we may have imagined. Importantly, it allows us to understand not only the end point of adopting a pedagogical model but also the "messy turns" (Cook, 2009, p. 282) inherent in pedagogical change. It allows us to map the notions of practice architectures, and pedagogical models as design specifications, against the main idea, critical elements and learning aspirations of different models as discussed in empirical research.

This chapter provides examples of what we can learn directly from the researchers and users of pedagogical models, unmediated by the reviewers of the research literature. We undertake this critical exploration with reference to how the *sayings*, *doings* and *relatings* of practice architectures inform the practice of pedagogical models (Kemmis, 2009; Kemmis et al., 2014). Specifically, we seek to highlight the *sayings*, *doings* and *relatings* of schools, in particular teachers, when it comes to changing practice and adopting an approach to teaching that uses pedagogical models. We get a closer and more micro look at what happens when a pedagogical model meets the reality of practice in schools.

Having undertaken this mapping, we explore the use of the term "hybrid models" and consider what it is about this notion that throws light on the practice architectures of pedagogical models more broadly. It is our belief that whilst we see a growing body of literature on hybridised models, many questions remain unanswered, not least those related to the nature of the hybrid that emerges from the conjoining of two individual models. We argue that true hybridisation rarely occurs, but instead a composite model (with two main ideas, two sets of critical elements, etc.) emerges from such a union of models. We argue that careful consideration needs to be given to the combination of different pedagogical models in terms of their signature practices architectures, and that authors need to establish the main idea(s), critical elements and learning aspirations of any composition of models to ensure the meaningful alignment of curriculum, teaching, learning and assessment.

We explore six empirical papers in this chapter. All six papers were chosen because they represent the uses of pedagogical models (sport education, teaching personal and social responsibility, tactical games, and cooperative learning), the uses of models in different contexts (pre-service teaching in Ireland, after-school clubs in the USA, national curriculum reform in Singapore, curriculum change in the UK, minority groups in the USA and high school students in Spain) or are examples of multi-model use or hybridisation. There are, of course, many other papers we might have explored and, in doing so, our consideration of practice architectures may have been different. We believe, however, that we while we might have seen differences, we might also have found similar broad-brush considerations of the main idea, critical elements, learning aspirations and pedagogy of each model. Nevertheless, these studies are a means to better understand how pedagogical models serve as design specifications for curriculum planning.

They help us explore the ways in which authors have, or indeed have not, used or adapted the main idea, critical elements, learning aspirations and pedagogy of each model in their respective study.

Pre-service teachers' use of sport education

In their paper, *The influence of organizational socialization in preservice teachers' delivery of sport education*, Deenihan and MacPhail (2017) explored the barriers and enablers of using sport education in Irish secondary schools. At the core of the paper is a reporting of the broader and context-specific practice architectures of using both MbP and a single pedagogical model. The reported *sayings* talk of a profession that lacks experience in using pedagogical models such as sport education, a fact that often leads teachers to abandon innovation pedagogy for the tried and tested safety of multi-activity, sport technique-based physical education. This broader practice architecture is both challenged and/or reinforced by the qualified teachers in schools. This happened because, while the majority of teachers associated with the study (both pre-service and qualified) lacked experience with sport education, some embraced change while others resisted it. However, there were also qualified teachers who initially supported change but later withdrew this support in favour of traditional teacher-led criteria when it came to judging the pre-service teachers' (PSTs) use of sport education. Although the PSTs had been introduced to sport education at university, the supporting teachers lacked a vocabulary for sport education to meaningfully support PSTs beyond encouragement. This lack of knowledge, language, understanding and experience (i.e. *sayings* and *doings*) limited the implementation of sport education in every school.

The wider *doings* of sport education, as reported in the cited literature, highlighted the importance of school-university partnership, recognised the difficulties PSTs had teaching what others have described as MBP (with no differentiation between single and multi-model MBP) and recommend that PSTs first teach sport education on teaching placement with university tutor support, all of which Deenihan and MacPhail (2017) did. The authors also recognised the wider political agenda (*relatings*) which had seen the development of "a new senior cycle physical education framework based on MBI [Model-Based Instruction]" (Deenihan & MacPhail, 2017, p. 479). Importantly, and despite this national policy change, none of the PSTs involved had experienced the senior cycle as school students themselves.

Notwithstanding national policy support, it was the difficulties in implementation that became the focus of the paper, with power over *doings* lying squarely with the schools and the supporting teachers and not with policy nor the PSTs. This was despite national and institutional agreement about the importance of a MBI approach, and sympathy from some teachers regarding the need to change and innovate. From a curriculum-as-design-specification perspective, PSTs were unable to use, or at least dissuaded from using, the critical elements of sport education, i.e. seasons, persisting teams, etc.

In one example, a supporting teacher felt it was appropriate to interfere during a PSTs' sport education class, interrupt the culminating event and openly disapprove of the lack of traditional, teacher-led practice. This enactment of power over the pedagogical choices of PSTs highlights a disparity between the *sayings, doings* and *relatings* of practice in some schools. Furthermore, it limited the capacity of sport education to serve as a design specification and instead shoehorned curriculum, teaching, learning and assessment into the more comfortable and familiar form of multi-activity, sport technique-based physical education. Other restrictions around what PSTs could do included the limitations inherent in a nine-week placement and other administrative burdens placed on individuals trying to qualify as teachers. The most prevalent *doings*, therefore, were controlled by supporting teachers and schools, especially when they operated in hierarchical power relations and enacted custodial practices.

The *relatings* of sport education showed that while the pedagogical model was seen to be beneficial to young people's development, its presence in school curricula diminished over time. In other words, it experienced initial success before petering out. This may have been a consequence of a lack of a working knowledge of sport education, a penchant for multi-activity, sport technique-based physical education, and/or an absence of innovative sites of practice for PSTs (Deenihan & MacPhail, 2017).

Despite the detail provided throughout, Deenihan and MacPhail's paper lacked any real sense of what sport education was outside of its name. The model was presented as a proper noun (see Casey, MacPhail, Larsson, & Quennerstedt, Online) and the reader was simply expected to understand sport education. There was no exploration of the main idea, the crucial elements or the learning aspirations, and the pedagogical expectations of curriculum, teaching, learning and assessment were not discussed. Indeed, the *doings* of these different sport education units jarred with the critical elements described by Hastie (2012) and others (e.g. Siedentop, 1994). For example, the nine-week placement determined that a season could not operate over the extended period of time expected. This, coupled with the requirement for sport education to fit into the current notion of physical education as a multi-activity, sport technique-based approach, probably contributed to the difficulties in implementation articulated in this paper.

After-school uses of teaching personal and social responsibility

In their exploration of S*ocial and emotional learning through a teaching personal and social responsibility based after-school programme*, Gordon, Jacobs, and Wright (2016) took explicit steps to articulate what we now recognise as the main idea, critical elements, learning aspirations and pedagogy (i.e. the curriculum, teaching, learning and assessment) of teaching personal and social responsibility. Despite referring to teaching personal and social responsibility as both an instructional model and MBP, notwithstanding that it is single model, Gordon et al. took the time to reason for its *sayings*, *doing* and *relatings*.

In regard to *sayings*, Gordon et al. (2016) argue that teaching personal and social responsibility addresses the recognised need for children and young people to "become better members of society" (p. 358) through the positioning of social and emotional competence as an educational outcome. Positioning teaching personal and social responsibility as an exponent of such outcomes, the authors maintained that the model was well-placed to achieve such aims. Such is the articulated importance of social and emotional development in the global language of education it was unsurprising that – at a local level – school leaders in this study were seen to endorse the extended use of teaching personal and social responsibility in both the afterschool and school settings.

Gordon et al. (2016) positioned the development of life skills and personal and social responsibility as more desirable *doings* of sport and activity-based programs than the traditional outcomes of competency and engagement inherent in multi-activity, sport technique-based physical education. Justifying such outcomes by national and state legislation, Gordon et al. supported, albeit unintentionally, Deenihan and MacPhail's (2017) call for university/school partnerships. Conversely, they also appeared to seek to teacher-proof the use of TPSR by not directly involving a school teacher in the running of the afterschool club. Despite this exclusion, Gordon et al. (2016, p. 365) reported that "high fidelity" (Hastie & Casey, 2014) to what we have positioned as the critical elements of TSPR helped the young people involved recognise, through self-awareness, their "emotions, strengths and weaknesses."

In adopting a broad focus around the need for young people to control their emotions, develop social skills and make healthy choices, Gordon and colleagues articulated the manner in which young people should *relate* to the world. These justifications are well-established in the physical education and sport pedagogy community's expectations as to how we expect young people to engage with each other and their environment. Whilst, as

Gordon et al. (2016) argue, such responsibilities lie across a multitude of subject areas, these *relatings* also talk loudly about the importance of developing life skills. Such a rationalisation for teaching personal and social responsibility is justified more broadly in the findings which celebrate discussion and considerations of self-awareness and challenge in group meetings and reflection times.

Throughout their work, Gordon et al. (2016, p. 360) clearly articulated the main idea of teaching personal and social responsibility (i.e. promotion of "social and personal development by shifting the focus of sport away from solely acquiring technical sport skills and adding an equal focus on developing personal and social responsibility"), the critical elements (i.e. "relational time, awareness talk physical activity lesson, group meeting, and reflection time") and the learning aspirations (i.e. respect, participation and effort, self-direction, leadership and transfer) they held for the model. In doing so, and in exploring implementation fidelity, they sought to ensure that any reader was well-versed in the version of teaching personal and social responsibility they used and its associated outcomes. Finally, taking a lens of pedagogy, the authors spoke of curriculum, teaching, learning and assessment in their paper. This open articulation of pedagogy further strengthens a reader's understanding of pedagogical model use; albeit that they used the moniker of instructional model and equated single model use to MbP.

The tactical approach in Singapore

Exploring the mandated inclusion of a tactical games approach in Singapore's physical education syllabus, Wright, McNeil, and Fry (2009) focused on the teaching, learning and mentoring perspectives of using a new pedagogical model. They positioned their study of curriculum renewal around the Singaporean government's drive to produce "critical and creative thinkers" (Wright et al., 2009, p. 223). Despite the *sayings* integral to this Government-led drive for change, Wright et al. relied more on the language of constructivism and situated learning than on tactical games. Arguing against the "corporality of the field of physical education" (p. 226) Wright and colleagues (2009, p. 227) posited that teachers need to make a conceptual leap from "traditional, transmission modes of teaching to more student-centred, constructivist approaches."

In narrowing their focus to the implementation of tactical games at a curriculum level, Wright et al. (2009) allowed us to see something of the localised practice architectures of the schools, student teachers and cooperating teachers involved in the study. These *doings* showed that real games – as previously experienced in the prevalent multi-activity, sport technique-based approaches – carried significant weight in the language and under-standing of students. Indeed, Wright et al. (2009, p. 236) held that student teachers had to "deconstruct this misrepresentation that modified games are not real and have no connection to the 'bigger' picture of codified games and sports."

Outside of proposing a different notion of *doing* physical education, one that would see students gradually take control of the curriculum and instruction at the behest and instigation of their teachers, Wright et al. had little to say about existing *doings* and *relatings* of practice that impacted on both teaching and learning in schools, and the need for country-wide pedagogical change. When considering implementation specifically, Wright et al. acknowledged the support for tactical games provided by the Ministry of Education. Finally, and in keeping with both Deenihan and MacPhail (2017) and Gordon et al. (2016), Wright et al. (2009) lauded the importance of university-school partnerships. They reasoned that such collaborations provided support in terms of coursework and learning relating to the rel-evant pedagogical model. Conversely, however, they argued that these were not as beneficial as *doing* tactical games "with students in 'authentic' school settings, rather than with their peers in the university setting" (p. 238).

The notion of *relatings* revolved around the teaching ability/competence of student teachers. Those expected to gain a distinction in their teacher edu-cation course gained better feedback from their students and helped them to see the social outcomes that could be achieved from tactical games. In contrast, "credit" student teachers talked more about games-concepts, and "pass" student teachers talked more about general games concepts. From a *sayings* perspective it almost seems obvious to suggest that "better" teach-ers were seen to do better with GCAs. Although *relatings* seemed to support this view, it is difficult to tell whether this outcome is genuine or "part of the *happening* that unfolds in a particular place" (Kemmis et al., 2014, p. 34, original emphasis).

Regardless of the "credit" level of the student teachers, the national drive for change through the implementation of a tactical games approach could have been structured either as a specification for practice or a prescribed list of content or teaching and learning experiences. As a specification for prac-tice, the tactical games approach would have been seen as provisional, in the sense that regular and ongoing adaptation of plans and programs would be necessary to meet new contingencies and sets of circumstances. As a prescribed list, it would strongly favour calls for teacher-proofing (Ball, 2017). While it is hard to ascertain from the paper the exact nature of the implementation, there are strong enough hints to suggest that it was more prescription than specification for practice. For example, in their discussions of teaching, Wright et al. (2009, p. 233) "revealed that the STs were able to actualise the GGA lesson structure." More telling, perhaps, was the finding that "the most prevalent hindrances to the STs' teaching of the GCA were logistical, with 33% complaining of a lack of facility space and a further 22% bemoaning a lack of equipment" (p. 234). Consequently, whilst we have envisioned pedagogical models as the foundational element of a MbP approach to program design, the Ministry of Education in Singapore saw it as a verbatim solution to problems they recognised in physical education. However, without local agency that sees school physical education programs based on pedagogical models constructed by teachers, students and other stakeholders at specific points in the program planning and implementation process, our notion of curriculum co-construction cannot be realised and, as such, MbP cannot be actualised.

A models-based approach to secondary physical education

In the first empirical paper of its kind, Casey and MacPhail (2018) explored a MbP approach to physical education. Investigating a multi-year, multi-model, multi-class implementation of three pedagogical models (cooperative learning, sport education and tactical games), these authors scrutinised pedagogical change from the vantage point of an experienced practitioner researcher (Casey himself). Casey and MacPhail (2018) used the notion of model fidelity (Hastie & Casey, 2014) to provide a rich description of the curricular elements (i.e. the main idea, critical elements, learning aspirations and pedagogy) of the three models explored in this paper.

Digging deeper and exploring each facet of practice architectures in turn, it is clear that Casey and MacPhail (2018) took a robust approach to positioning their work in the broader narratives of physical education and education. The *sayings* talked of agendas around student voice, the need to move beyond single model MbP and the need to help teachers (both pre-service and in-service) understand and gain experience and confidence in using multiple models in a program.

The authors argued that it was necessary to define the *doings* we aspire to in physical education and find approaches that best facilitate these ambitions. They position a MbP approach as a way of "meaningfully and purposefully connect[ing] different models in a school's curriculum" (Casey & MacPhail, 2018, p. 296). This was partially achieved in the results of the paper through the teacher's "continually striving for high fidelity" and his "knowledge of his classes" (p. 302). In keeping with MbP the researchers also reported on the teacher's predominantly/partially successful attempts to reduce his involvement and grant the students ownership over their learning. Casey showed authenticity as a teacher by trying to "squeeze every drop of time from the lesson" (p. 305) and his vulnerability by "trying to achieve too much in the time he had" (p. 305).

The *relatings* of study were used to show that the teacher's knowledge of both the class and the different pedagogical models was a strength of the curriculum. Casey and MacPhail (2018) acknowledged the importance of changing the power relationships in lessons and providing students with "the language and physical skills they would need to enact their roles effectively as well communicate with their peers and teacher" (p. 304). They also acknowledged the difficulties inherent in doing this and the amount of time required. Nevertheless, such a power shift changed the teacher's view of his students: "rather than products that I produce they are more like co-authors of their work works" (p. 306).

Fundamentally, Casey and MacPhail (2018) positioned each model as a specification for practice and showed how the curriculum was tailored to the local context. Equally they showed how pedagogical models could act as both a new organising centre for program design, and allow for the co-construction of physical education among teachers, students and stakeholders. Nevertheless, whilst this work gives us our first empirical example of MbP, this was a rudimentary attempt – by the standard we aspire to in Chapter 7 – that fitted into and around the multi-activity, sport technique-based approach to physical education that dominated the school's curriculum.

Summary

All four papers explored so far in this chapter have, to various degrees, highlighted the common and site (or at least study) specific practice architectures adopted when different pedagogical models are used. As such, they serve as proxies for the diverse range of approaches teachers and researchers and teacher-researchers and pre-service teachers take when they adopt different models. Significantly, while some authors showed the flexibility we would expect when a pedagogical model is seen as a design specification for the development of local curricula, Wright et al.'s (2009) paper showed the lack of distance teachers tolerated between the model blueprints and its implementation in local curricula.

In the next part of the chapter we consider what happens when hybrid or composite pedagogical models are used. Specifically, we ask: "What happens when we combine them in a curriculum?" We begin with an exploration of hybridisation and argue that there are few true hybrid models (which, in reality are new models) in physical education. Instead, what we have is a number of composite models. It would be appropriate to suggest that a teacher, with the support of their students and other stakeholders, could create a hybrid and that hybridisation, in such a case, would take place in local practice. However, when hybridisation is undertaken by researchers away from practice then it returns to the conceptual framework phase. In this way, and as Casey (2016) suggested, it is important that such models are constructed, not only through the ruminations of scholars, but also through testing, reflection and revision in practice contexts. We ultimately aspire for pedagogical models (hybrid or otherwise) to be design specifications that form the basis for the development of local programs.

Hybridisation and/or composition

The growing body of literature around hybrid models shows a level of adaptation and innovation that drives the field in different directions. That said, and as we will explain, when the lenses of pedagogical models and their respective practice architectures are applied to such a hybrid we start to see the emergence of a composite and not a hybrid model, with a handful of notable exceptions (see Ennis et al., 1999; Hastie & Buchanan, 2000; Luguetti, Oliver, Kirk, & Dantas, 2017). It is our belief that whilst we see a growing body of literature on hybridised models, many questions remain, not least those related to the nature of the hybrid that emerges from conjoining two individual models into one. Consequently, we argue that true hybridisation does not occur in the vast majority of cases, but instead a composite model emerges from such a union of models. Therefore careful consideration needs to be given to the combination of different pedagogical models, and authors need to establish the main ideas, critical elements and learning aspirations that govern any composition of models to ensure the meaningful alignment of teaching, learning, curriculum and assessment.

In the two sub-sections that follow, we explore two papers purporting to explore hybridised models. Whilst we will demonstrate what we regard quality in these papers, we support the concept and actualisation of hybridisation in one paper, and make an alternative case for a composition of pedagogical models in the second.

Hybridisation

In their work on seeking to improve the social environment in schools Ennis et al. (1999) developed a new hybrid pedagogical model from sport education. In *Creating a sense of family in urban schools using the "sport for peace" curriculum*, Ennis et al. (1999, p. 273) argued that the *sayings* around the model aspired to "learning in a socially satisfying setting" and focused on "enhancing personal and social identity." Specifically they argued that poverty and unemployment among young people, many of whom were from minority groups, had a negative impact on effort in the current milieu of schools. Consequently they held that there was a need for new forms of practice that focused on the most challenging school conditions and contexts. These conditions were made more difficult when students were aware of talk in their communities that suggested that, despite their attendance at school, they were unlikely to finish their studies and would, in all probability, experience a life of poverty and unemployment.

The implementation of the sport for peace curriculum, Ennis and colleagues argued, changed the *sayings* in the school. This was most obvious when the talked-about dominance of the most able boys was replaced with expectations around equitable engagement and shared responsibility. Furthermore, teachers' expectations about young people changed. Where students were once positioned as the problem, the sport for peace curriculum repositioned them as responsible individuals and groups who demonstrated camaraderie in their classes.

The biggest changes, however, occurred in *doings* and *relatings* of practice. From a *doings* perceptive, the broader aspiration was to create a school curriculum that encouraged young people to "interact respectfully over an extend time period" (Ennis et al., 1999, p. 273). Such *doings* were constrained by the lack of control teachers and schools had over the curriculum and testing standards, and the absence of teaching environments favourable to learning.

Whilst sport for peace did not change the physical space *per se*, it did change the way teachers and young people looked at and used that space. It created roles and responsibilities for students that were previously lacking and created opportunities and spaces in which teachers and students could share ideas and co-construct the curriculum. As the project developed through three reported phases of implementation, Ennis et al. observed teachers moving away from expectations of practice that required them to intervene promptly when conflict appeared to a sense and purpose that positioned young people as brokers of peace and not solely instigators of conflict. Consequently, teachers provided students with the tools and the autonomy to resolve their own disputes rather than reconfiguring lessons to keep potential antagonists apart.

Ennis et al. (1999, p. 273) argued that students from disadvantaged and challenging locations and populations could be helped to develop "social affiliation and achievement." Such individuals, who were most likely to come from single-parent families, previously experienced teaching that focused on the perceived need for teachers to establish power over their classes in an effort to maintain order and discipline. These *relatings* were one of the biggest obstacles going into this project, yet the research team resisted the temptation to "present scripted lessons or a lockstep approach to the curriculum" (Ennis et al., 1999, p. 276). Instead of teacher-proofing sport for peace, they empowered teachers to change these *relatings* through workshops and discussions around nego-tiations and compromise.

Where previously the *doings* of physical education in this context had given power to the higher ability male students, sport for peace shifted prac-tice so that "ability" became more about solidarity and the social spaces of lessons than being the best player. Indeed, as the three phases of sport for peace progressed, students were increasingly empowered to redress per-ceived imbalance:

> When players perceived that the ball was not distributed fairly to eve-ryone, they discussed the problem, expressed their feelings and per-suaded others that the current system was unjust.
>
> (Ennis et al., 1999, p. 280)

Significantly, the use of sport for peace encouraged teachers to share respon-sibility and ownership of the curriculum with their students; a process we recognise as a specification for practice rather than a prescribed list of con-tent or teaching and learning experiences. This allowed students to experi-ence game-based physical education from a different perspective, one that did not favour students for their skills alone:

> Highly skilled students were unable to gain respect through dominant play. Instead they earned respect through thoughtful decision making, effective teaching, and positive support of every player. They earned respect by solving problems and responding to their players' criticisms and settling disputes.
>
> (Ennis et al., 1999, p. 282)

That did not mean that this was a win-win situation. Indeed, and as Ennis and colleagues concluded:

> The decision to disrupt aggressive behaviours in physical education is a political and controversial one for some physical educators. Teachers who, themselves, have experienced success in these highly competitive

environments are sceptical of both the need to create a safe place and the process used to structure this environment.

(Ennis et al., 1999, p. 284)

Alongside the project of practice discussed in the paper, Ennis et al. (1999) also outlined the main idea, critical elements, learning aspirations and pedagogy inherent in sport for peace. The main idea of the model was to enhance and emphasise "the responsibility concept proposed by Siedentop (e.g. team affiliation, student ownership of teams and game schedules, sport roles) essential to developing peaceful relationships" (Ennis et al., 1999, p. 274). At its core the model had one key learning aspiration:

The sport for peace curriculum was designed to reflect the characteristics of peace education with goals and curricular structures specifically focused on promoting nonviolent behavior, a sense of community, and student ownership or empowerment within the school curriculum.

(Ennis et al., 1999, p. 274)

To achieve both the main idea and learning aspirations, sport for peace employed a number of critical elements: (a) all students must play in every lesson and for equal periods of time, (b) students must rotate through each position (in their playing role) and through each of the different organisational roles, and (c) in order to prepare for situations in which they would need to compromise and negotiate, students practiced and role-played conflict, game play and problem solving. Pedagogically, sport for peace moved away from multi-activity, sport technique-based physical education, in which student were exposed to the skills of the game, to one of equal opportunity and engagement. Whilst the context (i.e. basketball) remained unchanged, the assessment changed from one that valued skill to one that valued equity and inclusion. The teachers moved away from a fixed notion of teaching and learning that they controlled to one they co-constructed with their students and which was bespoke to their local context.

In (re)considering the sport for peace model through the lenses of practice architectures it is possible to imagine what hybrid pedagogical models can (and should) aspire to be. In many ways, this paper serves as exemplar of single model practice and of hybridisation. This was not sport education. Instead sport for peace was derived from sport education. The authors deliberately added a curriculum for global peace and, in doing so, they added a curricular emphasis on "conflict negotiation and care and concern for others" (p. 274) to create a new hybrid model.

Composition

The application of practice architectures to Fernandez-Rio and Menendez-Santurio's (2017) paper *Teachers and students' perceptions of a hybrid sport education and teaching for personal and social responsibility learning unit* highlights a range of *sayings* around curriculum, instructional and pedagogical models. Whilst they argue for a models-based approach, they repeated the now common argument that although MbP has a large body of supportive empirical research behind it, it isn't easy for teachers to learn "without the necessary support from model-makers and university researchers" (p. 185). In arguing for a hybrid model Fernandez-Rio and Menendez-Santurio presented an argument that no one model is capable of supporting learning in every facet of physical education. We have used this argument ourselves for MbP but believe that any hybrid/composite model is still a single model and, as such, falls short of the teaching, learning, curriculum and assessment requirements of the subject as a whole.

Early in the paper, Fernandez-Rio and Menendez-Santurio (2017) detailed the main ideas and critical elements of both sport education and teaching personal and social responsibility (TPSR). They also articulated the main ideas of these models respectively, but did not explain, for example, how the idea of providing "students with meaningful sporting experiences" (p. 185) complemented or changed the idea of "helping individuals acquire values and responsibilities through physical activity" (p. 186). Similarly, Fernandez-Rio and Menendez-Santurio (2017) explained the six basic elements of sport education and the five goal levels of teaching personal and social responsibility, but did not explain how they would be used together nor how the differences in aim and purpose were to be managed. In failing to do this, they either created a hybrid model with 11 critical elements, or a composite that utilised the perceived strengths of each model without acknowledging the inherent flaws or challenges of such an approach. How, for example, did Level 3 of the TPSR model (i.e. "self-direction: showing on-task interdependence, goal setting progression and courage to resist peer pressure" [Fernandez-Rio & Menendez-Santurio, 2017, p. 186]) impact (i.e. alter, detract or enhance) the third basic element of sport education (i.e. "formal competition: all through the season, teams compete against each other under different formats" (p. 185))? At first sight these could be complementary but, we would argue, they are certainly not neutral. If they did clash, which took precedence?

Gordon (2009) asked if the merging of teaching personal and social responsibility and sport education was *a marriage made in heaven or hell*, and argued that, despite the apparent congruence of the two models, "tensions can arise when the two [models] are taught as a merged model" (p. 14). He reasoned that when the requirements of one model diverged from the requirements of the other, one will win and its outcomes will consequently be strengthened while the outcomes relating to the other model will be weakened. To this end, Gordon (2009) emphasised the importance of consciously deciding which set of outcomes we wish to prioritise before we start to plan and teach:

> the strong suggestion is that they [teachers] make a conscious decision to prioritise one of the two models rather than attempting to meet the goals of both. In other words, teachers should decide whether they are teaching TPSR, with Sport Education being used as context, or they are teaching a Sport Education unit which includes some aspects of TPSR. This is not an equal merging of the two models but a situation in which elements of one are used to strengthen the outcomes related to the prioritised model. . . . This is a more favourable outcome than the alternative where neither model is consistently given priority. In this situation decision making can become reactive and inconsistent with a resulting weakening of learning for both models.
>
> (Gordon, 2009, p. 16)

From a *doings* and/or *relatings* perspective, Fernandez-Rio and Menendez-Santurio (2017), like Casey and MacPhail (2018), used the notion of model fidelity (Hastie & Casey, 2014) to show how the 16 lesson unit was structured to follow both the critical elements of sport education and teaching personal and social responsibility (including a learning unit plan). This level of detail is to be commended, but the focus on what was done (i.e. the *doings*) and the significance of noting "100% agreement" that "implementation [of each model] was correct" (i.e. the *relatings*), suggests that instead of creating a hybrid of two models, two models were used in their entirety. Nonetheless, nothing is mentioned about the consequence of, for example, "the teacher us[ing] direct instruction and learning cues" (Fernandez-Rio & Menendez-Santurio, 2017, p. 188). Does this indicate that a composite of two pedagogical models is not enough? How did the use of direct instruction change what happened in the intervention?

In their discussion, Fernandez-Rio and Menendez-Santurio (2017, p. 193) "revealed the value of combining the structural features of the Sport Education Model that students find so attractive (enjoyment) with the micro pedagogies of another model (Teaching for Personal and Social Responsibility) that provide teachers with attractive learning environments (teaching approach)." This value attribution speaks clearly about the *doings* at play in this approach but ignores the tensions that existed between "competition and cooperation" (Fernandez-Rio & Menendez-Santurio, 2017, p. 193). It also smooths over *relatings* that required compromise. Unlike sport for peace, where a new model was created, the "Sport Education + Teaching for Personal and Social Responsibility kickboxing learning unit" (p. 194) is, in our reading, a double-model composition in which both models coexist. While this clearly had a positive impact on the participants in the study it feels disingenuous to describe this, or indeed a number of other reported hybrids, as hybrids (see Casey and Dyson [2009] as another example of a composite).

Conclusion

In this chapter we have taken a micro view of both the features (main idea, critical elements, learning aspirations and pedagogies) and practice architectures (the *sayings*, *doings* and *relatings*) of a number of pedagogical models used in physical education. Although we acknowledge that these papers serve only as approximations of what people actually do with models, we believe they show the diversity of practice that comes about when teachers and researchers interpret and then implement pedagogical models. On the whole the main idea, critical elements, learning aspiration and pedagogies seen in Chapter 3 are present in these empirical studies. The *sayings*, *doings* and *relatings* likewise are recognisable. Conversely, there are differences between the aspirations of model-makers and the actualisations of teachers. These models are not realised as prescriptions but are instead, at least in the majority of cases, specifications that are then moulded to suit the site of practice and the people found there. As design specifications they allow for some local agency but it is here – when pedagogical models meet the reality of practice – that multi-activity, sport technique-based physical education exerts its power and distorts the aspirations of stakeholders and model-makers alike.

Taken together these papers suggest that pedagogical models can operate, at a local level, as design specifications for the development of programs and practice in local contexts. As such they can be considered, in Stenhouse's (1975, p. 142) terms, as "a way of translating any educational idea into a hypothesis testable in practice." The pedagogical models considered here are robust enough to withstand the test of practice, providing teachers and other stakeholders in a school community with sufficient guidance to create their own local curricula. The practice architectures of the pedagogical models explored in this chapter provide sufficient guidance to create quality physical education programs without prescribing in detail what teachers and students should do. Understandably, there is slippage between aspiration and actualisation. Also, there are residual and dominant practices and expectations to contend with.

What they represent instead, we will argue in the next chapter, is the basis for the construction and constitution of MbP. This and the previous chapter have shown how the signature practice architectures of selected pedagogical models become refracted through the writings of reviewers of the literature and through research on the implementation of single models. In the next chapter, we seek to show how the analyses in the three proceeding chapters informs a judgement about the extent to which these selected and other pedagogical models may be robust enough to realise the four core principles of pedagogical models we set out in Chapter 1, and thus to form a basis to take forward MbP in schools.

References

Ball, S. J. (2017). *The education debate* (3rd ed.). Bristol: Policy Press.
Casey, A. (2016). Models-based practice. In C. D. Ennis (Ed.), *Routledge handbook of physical education pedagogies* (pp. 54–67). London: Routledge.
Casey, A., & Dyson, B. (2009). The implementation of models-based practice in physical education through action research. *European Physical Education Review, 15*(2), 175–199.
Casey, A., & MacPhail, A. (2018). Adopting a models-based approach to teaching physical education. *Physical Education and Sport Pedagogy, 23*(3), 294–310.
Casey, A., MacPhail, A., Larsson, H., & Quennerstedt, M. (2020). Between hope and happening: Problematizing the M and the P in models-based practice. *Physical Education and Sport Pedagogy.* https://doi.org/10.1080/17408989.2020.1789576.
Cook, T. (2009). The purpose of mess in action research: Building rigour though a messy turn. *Educational Action Research, 17*(2), 277–291.
Deenihan, J. T., & MacPhail, A. (2017). The influence of organizational socialization in preservice teachers' delivery of sport education. *Journal of Teaching in Physical Education, 36*(4), 477–484.
Ennis, C. D., Solmon, M. A., Satina, B., Loftus, S. J., Mensch, J., & McCauley, M. T. (1999). Creating a sense of family in urban schools using the "sport for peace" curriculum. *Research Quarterly for Exercise and Sport, 70*(3), 273–285.
Fernandez-Rio, J., & Menendez-Santurio, J. I. (2017). Teachers and students' perceptions of a hybrid sport education and teaching for personal and social responsibility learning unit. *Journal of Teaching in Physical Education, 36*(2), 185–196.
Gordon, B. (2009). Merging teaching personal and social responsibility with sport education: A marriage made in heaven or hell? *ACHPER Australia Healthy Lifestyles Journal, 56*(3–4), 13–16.
Gordon, B., Jacobs, J. M., & Wright, P. M. (2016). Social and emotional learning through a teaching personal and social responsibility based after-school program

for disengaged middle-school boys. *Journal of Teaching in Physical Education*, *35*(4), 358–369.

Hastie, P. A. (2012). *Sport education: International perspectives*. London: Routledge.

Hastie, P. A., & Buchanan, A. M. (2000). Teaching responsibility through sport education: Prospects of a coalition. *Research Quarterly for Exercise and Sport*, *71*(1), 25–35.

Hastie, P. A., & Casey, A. (2014). Fidelity in models-based practice research in sport pedagogy: A guide for future investigations. *Journal of Teaching in Physical Education*, *33*, 422–431.

Kemmis, S. (2009). Action research as a practice-based practice. *Educational Action Research*, *17*(3), 463–474.

Kemmis, S., Wilkinson, J., Edwards-Groves, C., Hardy, I., Grootenboer, P., & Bristol, L. (2014). *Changing practices, changing education*. London: Springer.

Luguetti, C., Oliver, K. L., Kirk, D., & Dantas, L. (2017). Exploring an activist approach of working with boys from socially vulnerable backgrounds in a sport context. *Sport, Education and Society*, *22*(4), 493–510.

Lund, J., & Tannehill, D. (2005). *Standards-based physical education curriculum development*. Sudbury, MA: Jones & Bartlett Publishers.

Siedentop, D. (1994). *Sport education: Quality PE through positive sport experiences*. Champaign, IL: Human Kinetics.

Stenhouse, L. (1975). *An introduction to curriculum research and development*. London: Heinemann.

Wright, S., McNeill, M., & Fry, J. M. (2009). The tactical approach to teaching games from teaching, learning and mentoring perspectives. *Sport, Education & Society*, *14*(2), 223–244.

6 Reorganising physical education through pedagogical models

The possibility of MbP

Introduction

Aspiration lies at the heart of heart of this book. The hope and ambition, the desire even, for MbP. Aspiration also lies at the heart of pedagogical models. Siedentop, Bunker and Thorpe, and Hellison, for example, may not have set out to build pedagogical models – as we have recognised them in this book – but they had the aspiration to change physical education. They envisioned new possibilities regarding how young people learn, how they are assessed and the curriculum that we build around them. Some, like Siedentop (sport education and play theory), Oliver (activist approach and feminist and social justice theories) and Dyson and Casey (cooperative learning and social interdependence theory), took the theories of our field, and when these were lacking borrowed theories from other fields, and built their models. Others, like Hellison (teaching personal and social responsibility) and Bunker and Thorpe (teaching games for understanding), started with practice, applied theory, and built their models from there. In both scenarios, however, these models were created and developed in and out of school and/or after-school settings. They have been tempered in "gymnasia" and come to us as well articulated, if somewhat disparate ideas. These are the ideas that we see as the core of MbP.

Our purpose in this chapter is to ascertain if the signature practice architectures of pedagogical models are robust enough to create a realistic possibility of MbP in physical education. In Chapter 1 we positioned MbP as an alternative form of physical education, and described four principles that we believe pedagogical models offer: (1) a new organising centre for program design; (2) a design specifications for local practice; (3) a way of managing the tension between local agency and external support; and (4) help in the co-construction of physical education among teachers, students and stakeholders. Taking up these principles again – and building on our scrutiny of pedagogical models in preceding chapters – we assess the extent to which pedagogical models are both ready and appropriate for the task of reorganising physical education as MbP.

In the following sections we take the four core principles in turn, and examine how they are expressed at macro, meso and micro levels of discourse on pedagogical models. Through this analysis, we note the extent to which pedagogical models provide new and alternative discursive arrangements/vocabularies for talking and thinking about physical education and thereby provide a means for stakeholders to imagine new pedagogical possibilities (*sayings*). We also consider the ways in which pedagogical models productively and constructively reorder and reorganise existing activities associated with school physical education such as games and sports, exercise and so on (*doings*), while introducing novel activities (e.g. yoga, reflective practice, cooperative games). Furthermore, we note the potential many models have, since they focus specifically on the affective domain, for working with young people on matters such as motivation, resilience, responsibility, etc. (*relatings*). We conclude the chapter by considering which models should be selected at which stages of schooling? Are there developmental issues to consider? Are there issues of complementarity of models which could be paired (e.g. teaching games for understanding/sport education)?

A new organising centre for program design

If we consider pedagogical models from a macro perspective, then none of the aspirations (*sayings*) of the different models (or in the case of Game Centred approaches (GCAs) genre of models) are what we recognise as traditional. The mainstays of multi-activity, sport technique-based physical education, i.e. teacher-led, introductory units of skills and drills, are replaced with, for example, interaction and interdependence (cooperative learning), player development in its fullest sense (sport education), inquiry based in action, and listening to respond (activist approach). The focus on skill development as the main driver for physical education is replaced by a quest for understanding (GCAs), and social and affective development (teaching personal and social responsibility) (*doings*). These reconfigurations of *sayings* and *doings* have consequences for the pedagogical and other relationships that are possible in physical education settings, both between teachers and students, and among students (*relatings*).

The meso consideration of a pedagogical model as an organising centre is, we believe, skewed in particular directions by the popularity of a given model. Both sport education and GCAs enjoy a currency in the literature of physical education that establishes them in the practices of the field, even though they are often parachuted into multi-activity, sport technique-based physical education (*sayings* and *doings*). Consequently, in both Hastie, de Ojeda, and Calderón's (2011) and Harvey and Jarrett's (2014) reviews there is little consideration, or at least articulation, of the main constitutive elements of curriculum, teaching, learning and assessment among the studies they reviewed. As we argued in Chapter 1, these four elements are interactive and interdependent, and together offer the definition of pedagogy that we work with in this book. A main organising principle for MbP in physical education, then, is these four interactive and interdependent elements taken together. The absence in the meso scale of practice – at least in two popular models – of these four elements suggests some degree of refraction of curriculum messaging from the original formulations of the models to their appropriation by other researchers and their application in practice.

It is important to recall and question, however, the decision made by both Hastie et al. (2011) and Harvey and Jarrett (2014) to position sport education and GCAs respectively as achievers of the "traditional 'big 5' aims of PE" (Alexander & Luckman, 2001, p. 11) i.e., motor skill development, fitness, social development, values and attitudes, and knowledge and understanding. Since, as we have argued, pedagogical models each have their own learning aspirations, it is not clear how they might also seek to achieve these additional aims for learning. This is not to say that there can be no broad and overarching aims for learning in physical education. Indeed, in Chapter 1 we discussed the possibility of a salutogenic concept of health as a focus for a strengths-based approach to constructing a rationale for physical education's place in the school curriculum. But in programs informed by MbP, these learning aspirations, framed by this broader rationale, need to be aligned with the models being used. The "big 5" aims of physical education have no obvious theoretical foundation in the way that, for example, a salutogenic concept of health or the notion of social justice pedagogy do (Kirk, 2020).

Despite the shortcomings of evaluating the achievements of each of these pedagogical models according to the "big 5" aims, there is some evidence at the meso level that the different pedagogical models we explored in Chapter 4 provide signature practice architectures for MbP in physical education. For example, both Hastie et al. (2011) and Casey and Goodyear (2015) provide examples of how users of different models articulated curriculum, teaching, learning and assessment as the key elements of pedagogy. Equally, Hastie and Wallhead (2016, p. 390) recognised different ways in which "student competence, literacy and enthusiastic participation" were achieved in different contexts and with different groups of students.

The view from a micro level consideration of various models suggests that, through collaborations between teachers and researchers and/or schools and universities, pedagogical models can serve as organising centres for physical education. In the case of both Casey and MacPhail's (2018) work and Ennis et al.'s (1999) intervention, the models in question acted as organising centres for the construction of local programs. Indeed, in the latter study, sport for peace replaced multi-activity, sport technique-based physical education completely. However, in terms of Casey and MacPhail's use of pedagogical models, this was fitted in alongside the multi-activity, sport technique-based approach that dominated the rest of the school's physical education program.

At the micro level, both Deenihan and MacPhail (2017) and Wright, McNeil, and Fry (2009) noted that a lack of experience with particular models, resistance from the school and its teachers, and issues of power, have the capacity to undermine the potential of a pedagogical model to become an organising centre for physical education. In both cases, even when a model's implementation was lauded in the beginning, existing power structures and approaches soon reimposed themselves. For instance, Wright et al. (2009, p. 227) argued that teachers needed to make a conceptual leap from "traditional, transmission modes of teaching to more student-centred, constructivist approaches." We would add a need for teachers not to leap back into tradition. Conversely, in Gordon, Jacobs, and Wright's (2016) paper the school itself recognised that young people's learning should be related to the "real world" and, to achieve this, they understood that they needed to change physical education. The majority of authors called for school and university partnerships to support model implementation and sustainability. This call reinforces our view that partnerships of agents internal and external to the school form an irreducible unit for curriculum innovation and development.

With the exception of Casey and MacPhail's (2018) exploration of MbP – and even then that was a multi-model approach wedged into a curriculum dominated by a multi-activity, sport technique-based curriculum – all of these examples explore the use of one model, even the combined model explored by Fernandez-Rio and Menendez-Santurio (2017) which we argued became a single approach. That said, there is evidence across the different levels of practice that a pedagogical model can become a new organising centre for a MbP approach to physical education.

Pedagogical models as design specifications

Across Chapters 3, 4 and 5 we provided a plethora of examples of pedagogical models as design specifications. The macro view offered in Chapter 3 is indicative of a comparable desire in model-makers to eradicate the focus on content as the organising principle which is characteristic of multi-activity, sport technique-based programs and explore instead, for example, game literacy (sport education) or games as a malleable form that shifts with the actions, decisions and understanding of the player (GCAs). Equally pedagogical models might see thinking and problem solving (cooperative learning, activist, GCAs, sport education) replace replication (multi-activity, sport-technique physical education), and allow teaching to shift from being teacher-centred to being student-centred, at least in aspiration. The dominance of learning in the physical domain (multi-activity, sport-technique physical education) is replaced with a desire to facilitate learning across other domains of learning such as the cognitive, social and affective (activist, cooperative learning). Student are asked to develop their own self-body-world connection and take responsibility for their actions (teaching personal and social responsibility).

When we move to the meso view, we see a change in the conceptualisation of pedagogical models as design specifications. Some reviewers engage in an exercise of "this approach is better than that approach." Normally, this is aimed at multi-activity, sport technique-based physical education but not always. This comparative approach is evidenced, for example, in sport education where the model is shown not only to enhance traditional outcomes such as motor development, performance and fitness but also tactical knowledge, social development and student attitudes and values (Hastie et al., 2011). In GCAs, there is a consideration of games being subject to cultural interpretation which, in turn, affects the experiences of participants. By contrast, there are clearer articulations around the aspiration of both cooperative learning and teaching personal and social responsibility and an acknowledgement of ways in which each model offers itself as a strategy for practice rather than a prescription (Casey & Goodyear, 2015; Richards & Shiver, Ahead of Print).

At the micro level of implementation, for example in both Deenihan and MacPhail's (2017) and Wright et al.'s (2009) studies, there were challenges to pre-service teachers' understanding of respective models. The lack of understanding of qualified teachers was also a challenge to model use, especially as they had the choice to stop participating or seriously change the use of the model. A lack of a working knowledge of models was more likely to contribute to a situation in which pedagogical models were misunderstood as prescriptions for practices, as programs in themselves, and not as design specifications (Deenihan & MacPhail, 2017; Wright et al., 2009). From a view of pedagogical models as design specifications, pre-service teachers were unable to use, or at least dissuaded from using, the critical elements of sport education, e.g. seasons, or persisting teams. Where qualified teachers had poor understanding of a model this led them to view the model as a prescription for practice and as a consequence were less likely to implement the model faithfully and more likely to omit one or more critical elements.

A core component of our aspiration to move away from multi-activity, sport technique-based physical education and the use of single models within multi-activity, sport technique-based physical education is the idea that pedagogical models serve as design specification for practice. Seen collectively, these three levels of macro, meso and micro discourse show both an aspiration to present pedagogical models as specifications and a degree of challenge at both meso and micro levels to realise this ambition. Given that pedagogical models are a key mechanism for managing the tension between external prescription and local agency there is a worry that when these different facets are not understood or are poorly understood, then the entire project of MbP is undermined. Either way, the adoption of MbP requires careful consideration and planning:

> it is important to consider how such a multiple models-based approach will work. Will, perhaps, teachers teach skill/games in the fall through Sport Education, fitness in the spring (through Health-Based Physical education or Fitness and Wellness) and leadership through (Adventure Education or Cooperative Learning) in the summer? . . . the use of multiple models in a curriculum will need careful consideration.
>
> (Casey, 2016, p. 62)

Local agency

At the macro level, the aspirations of the model-makers, collectively and individually, are for grassroot development. Each showed a concern in their writing for the learner (individually) and the adaptability of the setting in which they learn rather than content (i.e. skill and/or team games). Teachers are positioned as guardians of a healthy and safe participatory sport culture (for example, in sport education) where students share responsibility for planning and understanding the consequences of their in-game actions (GCAs). There is a desire across the models to move beyond nationally (or even internationally) recognised skills attainment and towards student-centred inquiry-based-in-action education (activist approaches) in which students learn with, by, from and for each other (cooperative learning). Student life skills, responsibility, self-awareness, self-management (teaching personal and social responsibility) and knowledge are redeveloped in collaboration with others (activist approaches). In the practising model (Aggerholm, Standal, Barker, &

Larsson, 2018), as an example of a new pedagogical model, agency is listed as one of the critical elements. In short, the knowledge that is valued by many model-makers is about self and others and not about skills and drills.

In considering the meso level through the lens of practice architectures, there is a clear indication that different models are focused on disrupting practice traditions and landscapes whilst simultaneously finding new sites of practice (sport education). There is little doubt that practice has been developing over time. Sport education, GCAs and teaching personal and social responsibility have a heritage of empirical research spanning many decades and cooperative learning, although a more recent addition to physical education in comparison, traces its origins still further back. The body of literature examined showed us that the signature practice architectures of these models have changed and evolved over time. That does not mean there are no challenges to be addressed or questions to be answered. In GCAs, for example, there are trials around the way questioning (of students and contexts) occurs and how modified games are developed to fit the local milieu. There are questions about the suitability of models and practices to teach across different domains of learning (cooperative learning). Equally, there is a consistency in the drive to put children first, and to explore and take responsibility for the unknowns.

At a micro level there appear to be challenges to local agency for preservice teachers. The power in the physical education department, as Rossi, Hunter, Christensen, and Macdonald (2015) highlight, lies with qualified rather than qualifying teachers. In short, qualified teachers do what needs to be done and pre-service and beginning teachers are expected to do the same. Consequently, it is unsurprising to read that the gift of local agency sits with the already powerful, with those already in the know. Equally, decisions made at a national level – as with the case of the Irish Senior Cycle and the Singapore government – still have to filter through the department. While the pre-service teachers in Deenihan and MacPhail's (2017) study had to endure interference, interruption and criticism, pre-service teachers in other studies were supported by their schools and colleagues to make change. In some cases (see Casey & MacPhail, 2018; Ennis et al., 1999) qualified teachers were able to reduce their involvement in lessons and grant students increased ownership over their learning experiences. Furthermore, local agency was experienced as bespoke learning tailored to the local context in which students were no longer seen as the problem but were instead positioned as responsible individuals who could interact respectfully over an extended period.

Viewing scales of practice across macro, meso and micro considerations of local agency allows us to see that while established teachers are positioned by model-makers as guardians of a healthy and safe participatory sport culture, there is little flexibility afforded to beginning teachers. In many cases there is evidence of confusion and power dynamics that act as barriers to local agency. It is only when the teacher has autonomy, or university-based teacher educators exert power themselves (for example, through requests that pedagogical models are used), that agency is possible. That said, and given that MbP requires departmental buy in as a minimum, there are indicators that local agency is both an attainable and appropriate principle.

The co-construction of physical education

At the macro level it is clear that the primary driver in each of these models is student-centred, age-appropriate physical education. There are clear statements in the *sayings* of different models that students are not young adults and they should not play adult games (sport education and GCA) or develop adult responses (cooperative learning, activist approaches, teaching personal and social responsibility). The relationships the young people create should be with themselves, their peers and/or the developmentally appropriate game, and not skills and drills taken from the adult game. The student is not the receiver of adult game knowledge and skills, or of activities to be experienced in the hope they will find something that interests them. Instead, in GCAs for example, they experience the game form at a developmentally appropriate level and work with their teachers and peers as the primary means of learning.

At the meso level, our consideration of the practice architectures of different models showed the spread of models from university departments (with their conceptual frameworks and models) into local curricula and back again. There is an increasing prevalence of studies exploring the use by researchers, pre-service and qualified teachers of pedagogical models with primary/elementary, secondary/high school and university student and/or students with special educational needs and disabilities. There is consideration of conceptual and instructional difficulties, time constraints and pedagogy. There are concerns around power dynamics when winning is positioned as the most important thing and when player autonomy leads to a reduction in a coach's authority (GCAs). There is a clear desire to explore and prioritise different domains of learning (cooperative learning and teaching personal and social responsibility) and challenges in overcoming the prevalence of short lessons, short blocks of work and large class sizes. While these debates do not present pedagogical models as the answer to all of the problems with multi-activity, sport technique-based physical education, they do highlight the focus on co-construction and indicate that this is one of a number of potential futures that physical education should continue to consider and develop.

Teachers served as the gatekeepers of co-construction of physical education at the micro level. When the teacher was required to step back from directive teaching, as with teaching personal and social responsibility, students were more involved in recognising their emotions, strengths and weaknesses. While involvement in pedagogical models is endorsed by school leaders, we do not advocate the teacher proofing inherent in Gordon et al.'s (2016) paper. Quite the opposite. Nonetheless, when a model's signature practice architectures required teachers to use alternatives to the directive teaching style, then they were able to position students "more like co-authors of their work" (Casey & MacPhail, 2018, p. 306) than passive recipients of innovative practice. When, as was the case of sport for peace, the model was built for the local context (as we would envision for MbP) young people were seen as brokers of peace and they were encouraged to share responsibility and ownership of the curriculum with their teachers. Such an outcome lies at the heart of our advocacy for MbP in physical education.

Summary

Despite these transformational aspirations [read pedagogical models], however, classrooms and schools have remained strikingly stable as social forms, still clearly recognisable as the progeny of the late nineteenth century multi classroom, multi teacher schools created in the industrial era and transported around the globe.

(Kemmis et al., 2014, p. 1)

With the exception of Ennis et al.'s (1999) sport for peace approach, pedagogical models are most frequently used alongside or within multi-activity, sport technique-based programs. Consequently, and as we will pick up in Chapter 7, they are constrained by what Kirk (2010, p. 49) describe as "a foundationalist, linear and hierarchical approach in which advanced skills are added on to the basic skills and tactics are learned after skills have been mastered at a level that enables a game to be played." It is important, therefore, that we consider the constraints and traditional expectations under which pedagogical models have been most often used and the many positives that have been reported.

Despite the enduring influence of sport technique-based programs, on the basis of our scrutiny of various pedagogical models in the preceding chapters and above, we believe that pedagogical models are appropriate for the task of reorganising physical education as MbP. We have shown the extent to which existing and emerging pedagogical models provide new and alternative discursive arrangements and provide new vocabularies for talking and thinking about physical education. We have discussed the means pedagogical models provide for stakeholders to imagine new possibilities for physical education. We have shown some of the ways in which pedagogical models productively and constructively reorder and reorganise existing activities associated with school physical education such as games, sports and exercise and allow teachers to introduce novel activities and outcomes into their programs. We also note the potential many models have, since they focus specifically on the affective domain, for working with young people on matters such as motivation, resilience and responsibility.

Fundamentally, we speak with confidence when we claim that pedagogical models offer (1) a new organising centre for program design; (2) can act as design specifications for local practice; (3) are capable of managing the tension between local agency and external support; and (4) allow for the co-construction of physical education among teachers, students and stakeholders. As such we state our claim that MbP is a viable future for physical education. However, we do so with an acknowledgement of the hard work needed to make it happen and the aspiration that such effort can changing the current cycle where:

> Tomorrow's world will pick up where today's left off, with the chairs in the places in the classroom where we left from yesterday, with the next chapter of the book from yesterday's lesson awaiting us, as with the football teams at the same place in the league table as well we went to bed last night.
>
> (Kemmis et al., 2014, p. 2)

A models-based practice approach to physical education

We think there already exist a sufficient number of pedagogical models, recast in the ways in which we have recommended in earlier chapters in this book, to constitute and construct MbP in physical education. The question then arises, what might this reconstruction look like on the ground? Which models might be best suited to particular education systems, particular schools, and particular groups of students? What might be the implications of MbP for school timetables, curriculum planning, teacher professional learning and assessment of pupil learning. Some of these questions we address in Chapter 7, where we consider the conditions that will need to be in place for the aspiration for MbP to become a reality. In the final section of this chapter, we consider the sequencing and developmental issues for MbP, and the extent to which models might be used together in complementary ways.

Some of the most popular models in terms of the regularity and frequency of their use in schools and other pedagogical settings, such as GCAs, sport education, and cooperative learning, have been implemented and studied in both primary and secondary school settings (Casey & Dyson, 2009; Casey, 2012, 2013; Dyson & Casey, 2016; MacPhail, Kirk, & Griffin, 2008; MacPhail, Kirk, & Kinchin, 2004). Activist approaches to working with girls in physical education have been used successfully in both upper primary and secondary schools (Oliver & Kirk, 2015). Other models would appear to be more developmentally appropriate to particular stages of schooling. For example, a model for the development of physical literacy through fundamental motor skills (Brian, Goodway, Logan, & Sutherland, 2017) might be ideally suited to an early years' phase in schooling. A model for health-based physical education, on the other hand, may be better placed in the secondary school (Haerens, Kirk, Cardon, & Bourdeauhuji, 2011). A proposed model for outdoor adventure activities may be more likely to be implemented in the secondary school setting (Williams & Wainwright, 2014a, 2014b) while a practising model (Aggerholm et al., 2018) could be used across the spectrum of education. Some models seem to operate in pedagogical settings out of regular school curriculum times, such as teaching personal and social responsibility (Richards & Shriver, Ahead of Print) and activist approaches to working with socially vulnerable youth (Luguetti, Kirk, & Oliver, 2019).

The order in which children and youth experience these and other models might, then, be determined by developmental issues. Order and sequencing may also be driven by pedagogical concerns. For example, would it benefit learners to experience a game-centred model prior to engaging in sport education? Clearly, a model for physical literacy could occur anywhere in the curriculum but might be more foundational than other models and should be experienced earlier on. Activist approaches to working with girls, in particular, may work well in the upper primary and lower secondary school levels when girls are most likely to be becoming disengaged from physical education.

Beyond these developmental and pedagogical considerations, we think that the ordering and sequencing of models may best be determined at local level, strategically, in consideration of the specific needs and interests of young people and their teachers and other stakeholders. We see no reason why some models could not be repeated at different levels of schooling. That said, we would urge against the use of only a small number of models, since we agree with a principle that has long informed multi-activity, sport technique-based approaches that some breadth of experience of the rich physical culture of societies is important. Multi-activity, sport technique-based physical education, in our view, often sacrifices depth for breadth. There would need to be considerable thought given, then, to how many models might be deployed in physical education programs and how often young people might encounter them.

Conclusion

> Education and schooling cannot be other than what they were yesterday and what they are today unless there are some significant transformations of the practices that reproduce and reconstitute schooling as we know it. Education and schooling will not be equal to the new historical challenges of the 21st-century, that is, if we cannot discover, develop and sustain changed and new practices of education.
>
> (Kemmis et al., 2014, p. 3)

Pedagogical models represent the significant transformations Kemmis and colleagues aspire to but there is a way to go if we wish to overwrite multi-activity, sport technique-based physical education with MbP. That said, and as we have shown, pedagogical models do have signature practice architectures. These will allow pedagogical models to become the organising centres for program design because they act as design specifications for local practice. Such signature practice architectures help stakeholders manage the tension between local agency and external prescription because they offer practitioners and other stakeholders room for manoeuvre (Priestley, Edwards, Priestley, & Miller, 2012), and allow for the co-construction of physical education among teachers, students, and stakeholders.

Having established in this chapter the extent to which pedagogical models might be fit for purpose in order to construct and constitute MbP in physical education, we now move in the next chapter to consider the conditions that we think will need to be in place in order for the possibilities inherent in this approach to be realised. Our overarching aspiration is that MbP facilitates the collaboration of teachers, students and other local stakeholders with researchers and other agents external to the school, each as necessary contributors to this process.

References

Aggerholm, K., Standal, O., Barker, D. M., & Larsson, H. (2018). On practising in physical education: Outline for a pedagogical model. *Physical Education and Sport Pedagogy, 23*(2), 197–208.

Alexander, K., & Luckman, J. (2001). Australian teachers' perceptions and uses of the sport education curriculum model. *European Physical Education Review, 7*(3), 243–267.

Brian, A., Goodway, J. D., Logan, J. A., & Sutherland, S. (2017). SKIPing with teachers: An early years motor skill intervention. *Physical Education and Sport Pedagogy, 22*(3), 270–282.

Casey, A. (2012). A self-study using action research: Changing site expectations and practice stereotypes. *Educational Action Research, 20*(2), 219–232.

Casey, A. (2013). "Seeing the trees not just the wood": Steps and not just journeys in teacher action research. *Educational Action Research, 21*(2), 147–163.

Casey, A. (2016). Models-based practice. In C. D. Ennis (Ed.), *Routledge handbook of physical education pedagogies* (pp. 54–67). London: Routledge.

Casey, A., & Dyson, B. (2009). The implementation of models-based practice in physical education through action research. *European Physical Education Review, 5*(2), 175–199.

Casey, A., & Goodyear, V. A. (2015). Can cooperative learning achieve the four learning outcomes of physical education? A review of literature. *Quest, 67*(1), 56–72.

Casey, A., & MacPhail, A. (2018). Adopting a models-based approach to teaching physical education. *Physical Education and Sport Pedagogy, 23*(3), 294–310.

Deenihan, J. T., & MacPhail, A. (2017). The influence of organizational socialization in preservice teachers' delivery of sport education. *Journal of Teaching in Physical Education, 36*(4), 477–484.

Dyson, B., & Casey, A. (2016). *Cooperative learning in physical education and physical activity: A practical introduction.* London: Routledge.

Ennis, C. D., Solmon, M. A., Satina, B., Loftus, S. J., Mensch, J., & McCauley, M. T. (1999). Creating a sense of family in urban schools using the "sport for peace" curriculum. *Research Quarterly for Exercise and Sport, 70*(3), 273–285.

Fernandez-Rio, J., & Menendez-Santurio, J. I. (2017). Teachers and students' perceptions of a hybrid sport education and teaching for personal and social responsibility learning unit. *Journal of Teaching in Physical Education, 36*(2), 185–196.

Gordon, B., Jacobs, J. M., & Wright, P. M. (2016). Social and emotional learning through a teaching personal and social responsibility based after-school program for disengaged middle-school boys. *Journal of Teaching in Physical Education, 35*(4), 358–369.

Haerens, L., Kirk, D., Cardon, G., & Bourdeauhuji, I. (2011). The development of a pedagogical model for health-based physical education. *Quest, 63*, 321–338.

Harvey, S., & Jarrett, K. (2014). A review of the game-centred approaches to teaching and coaching literature since 2006. *Physical Education and Sport Pedagogy, 19*(3), 278–300.

Hastie, P. A., de Ojeda, D. M., & Calderón, A. (2011). A review of research on sport education: 2004 to the present. *Physical Education and Sport Pedagogy, 16*(2), 103–132.

Hastie, P. A., & Wallhead, T. (2016). Models-based practice in physical education: The case for sport education. *Journal of Teaching in Physical Education, 35*(4), 390–399.

Kemmis, S., Wilkinson, J., Edwards-Grove, C., Hardy, I., Grootenboer, P., & Bristol, L. (2014). *Changing practices, changing education*. Singapore: Springer.

Kirk, D. (2010). *Physical education futures*. London: Routledge.

Kirk, D. (2020). *Precarity, critical pedagogy and physical education*. London: Routledge.

Luguetti, C., Kirk, D., & Oliver, K. L. (2019). Towards a pedagogy of love: Exploring pre-service teachers' and youth's experiences of an activist sport pedagogical model. *Physical Education and Sport Pedagogy, 24*(6), 629–646.

MacPhail, A., Kirk, D., & Griffin, L. (2008). Throwing and catching as relational skills in game play: Situated learning in a modified game unit. *Journal of Teaching in Physical Education, 27*(1), 100–115.

MacPhail, A., Kirk, D., & Kinchin, G. (2004). Sport education: Promoting team affiliation through physical education. *Journal of Teaching in Physical Education, 23*(2), 106–122.

Oliver, K. L., & Kirk, D. (2015). *Girls, gender and physical education: An activist approach*. London: Routledge.

Priestley, M., Edwards, R., Priestley, A., & Miller, K. (2012). Teacher agency in curriculum-making: Agents of change and spaces for manoeuvre. *Curriculum Inquiry, 42*(2), 191–214.

Richards, K. A. R., & Shiver, V. N. (Ahead of Print). "What's worth doing?": A qualitative historical analysis of the TPSR model. *Journal of Teaching in Physical Education*.

Rossi, T., Hunter, L., Christensen, E., & Macdonald, D. (2015). *Workplace learning in physical education: Emerging teachers' stories from the staffroom and beyond*. London: Routledge.

Williams, A., & Wainwright, N. (2014a). A new pedagogical model for adventure in the curriculum: Part 1 – advocating for the model. *Physical Education and Sport Pedagogy, 21*(5), 481–500.

Williams, A., & Wainwright, N. (2014b). A new pedagogical model for adventure in the curriculum: Part 2 – outlining the model. *Physical Education and Sport Pedagogy, 21*(6), 589–602.

Wright, S., McNeill, M., & Fry, J. M. (2009). The tactical approach to teaching games from teaching, learning and mentoring perspectives. *Sport, Education & Society, 14*(2), 223–244.

7 What conditions need to be in place for models-based practice to become a reality in physical education?

Introduction

Books such as this and others that seek to analyse current pedagogical practices in school physical education and other related pedagogical sites, and to propose and advocate for alternative ideas, will not change practice by themselves. We consider the research literature, of which this book is part, as necessary for the process of change, but not sufficient in itself. We need good ideas for and evidence of alternative practices that work to enhance the physical education of young people. We think this literature is relevant to change only when consideration is given to the conditions required for alternative forms of physical education such as MbP to take root and flourish. In the final chapter of this book, our purpose is to begin to sketch a route map of what needs to be done in order to take these ideas forward into tangible innovative actions in schools and other places where physical education is practiced.

So we ask the question, what would it take for MbP as we have defined it in this book to become a reality, as one way to remake school physical education so that it is fit for purpose and in better shape to realise the potential it clearly has for a broad range of educational and other benefits for young people? What conditions would need to be in place to facilitate and support pedagogical models as the organising centres for physical education programs? Who are the key stakeholders for making this happen? And what might be their roles and responsibilities? How might researchers, teachers, policymakers and students work together to implement and sustain MbP in and beyond schools?

We think, at one level, that MbP implies radical reform in the sense that it requires some quite different ways of thinking about, planning and providing for, and supporting, programs of physical education. As radical reform, some physical educators may approach this notion of MbP with caution, possibly with trepidation, others might see the challenge as insurmountable, and others may still dispute our critique of current practice set out in Chapters 1 and 2 and urge against such wholesale change.

While we believe there are radical elements to the adoption of MbP, we also think many of the conditions required to implement this reform are already in place. Some of these conditions will offer greater challenges to establish and sustain than others. For example, issues we will discuss below such as timetabling and national curricula are not necessarily within the remit of teachers, researchers or their national associations and organisations, and will need careful consideration and negotiation locally and further afield. Other issues, such as the specialist facilities available for teaching and learning in physical education, are already available to use, such as multi-purpose spaces and flexible equipment. Matters we also discuss below, such as a consensus on educational purposes, teacher professional learning, and the development of local collaborative hubs and district and national networks – while by no means easily created and sustained – are nevertheless well within our direct influence to shape according to our vision for a MbP future.

We present this chapter as an initial route map towards a MbP future for physical education. It is by no means complete, and needs to be tested, along with the rest of the proposals made in this book, by practice. We intend it to form the basis for an ongoing discussion among physical educators and our collaborators of how we might make MbP a reality in physical education, as one possible alternative to current practice.

Time and the timetable

The timetable is a common feature of educational institutions all over the world and at all levels of education systems. As the main means of setting out the order, sequencing, and duration of learning experiences, the timetable is a crucially important consideration in most attempts at educational innovation. And yet, for all of its importance, the timetable rarely features in the educational research literature. This is not to say that the timetable is never mentioned. It is, but only because it is such a fundamental feature of the ways in which schools, for example, organise themselves. When it is referred to as the main topic of discussion, it is most often treated as a technical problem to be resolved through the application of technology and algorithms. The ways in which the timetable operates, particularly in secondary schools, is rarely questioned in terms of its pedagogical effects on both teachers and students.

Chanan and Gilchrist, writing in the mid 1970s, highlighted a number of issues with the normative approach to timetabling in the secondary school, which they characterised as "the musical-chairs timetable":

> The conventional musical-chairs timetable is based on an assumption of a norm of pupil passivity and recalcitrance. Pupils have to be told what to do; they cannot be trusted; they do not want to learn; they have to be made to learn; this involves imposed discipline; they don't like discipline and are liable to rebel; they therefore need constant supervision. Professing to cope with this situation, the timetable exacerbates it. Sustained concentration, rhythmic development of learning to a natural climax, is impossible. At the sound of the bell, everything must change – the room, the subject, the teacher, sometimes the group. Half the energy of every lesson is taken up by the attempt to establish borders, procedures, norms for an arbitrary unit which will be abandoned again in a few moments. The overriding criterion of timetable planning is to make sure that all classes are occupied in all contact hours. The effect of adjacent lessons on each other, the effect of the cumulative sequence of lessons, is not considered. . . . The overall effect is an imposed superficiality, a self-fulfilling prophecy of pupil passivity, uninvolvement, restlessness and all that follows.
>
> (Chanan & Gilchrist, 1974, p. 16)

This is damning criticism. Their point is clear. Organisational issues dominate, and the matter of effective learning is a minor concern at best. Although it was made almost half a century ago, we might ask whether much has changed, at least in secondary schools in the UK. Indeed, it may be that high stakes examination's continuing dominance of the secondary school curriculum only serves to entrench this musical-chairs approach to timetabling.

This is not just a problem in UK secondary schools. In his book about teaching in New York, Gatto (1993) echoes Chanan and Gilchrist.

> When I'm at my best I plan lessons very carefully . . . But when the bell rings I insist they drop whatever it is we have been doing and proceed quickly to the next workstation. They must turn on and off like a light switch. Nothing important is ever finished in my class nor in any class I know of. Students never have a complete experience . . . Indeed, the lesson of bells is that no work is worth finishing, so why care too deeply about anything? . . . Bells [i.e. the timetable] are the secret logic of school time, their logic is inexorable. Bells destroy the past and future,

rendering every interval the same as any other, as the abstraction of a map renders every living mountain and river the same, even though they are not.

(Gatto, 1993, pp. 5–6)

Timetabling in primary schools has a somewhat different character to these descriptions of secondary schools, since students remain in the same class grouping for much of the school day. Nevertheless, while they may not change rooms or teachers for different school subjects, there is a process of ordering and sequencing particular curriculum topics throughout the school day. The logic of this process may be determined by district or national curriculum policy, or it may be informed by more local factors. For an example of the latter, in research on daily physical education in Queensland primary schools in the 1980s, teachers' timetabling decisions were determined by a need to keep children alert, or by the weather (Tinning & Kirk, 1991). In the case of the former, physical education often took place mid-morning between numeracy and literacy lessons and gave children a chance, as the teachers saw it, to burn-off excess energy and to aide their concentration. This was most likely to be in the months of cooler weather. In summer, physical education was often timetabled as the last session of the day so that sweaty children could be sent home directly after their lesson (Tinning & Kirk, 1991).

Predating Chanan and Gilchrist by just over a decade, Dave Munrow, at the time Director of Physical Education at the University of Birmingham in England, observed that even for the multi-activity, sport-based form of physical education that was emerging in the post-WWII era, the musical-chairs timetable characteristic of secondary schools of the time presented a serious challenge.

Any headmaster (sic) must feel somewhat bewildered at the prospect of timetabling a 'subject' the requirement for which may vary between twenty minutes on a squash court, an hour on the track, an hour and a half on the pitch and two days in the local hills or estuary. . . . The headmaster who is sympathetic to a catholic concept of physical education is still confronted by a total timetable in which every other subject is accustomed to fitting tidily into the units of single or double periods: and these are the subjects on which his school is primarily judged.

(Munrow, 1963, p. 273)

Kirk's (2010) analysis of the dominance of the multi-activity, sport technique-based approach to physical education shows that it is the musical-chairs timetable in secondary schools, where the majority of specialist physical education provision is based, that enables this form of physical education to persist, despite its many failings.

We suggest that the timetable presents similar challenges to MbP in physical education as the multi-activity, sports technique-based approach. The implementation of some pedagogical models in particular presents challenges for the musical-chairs timetable. For example, sport education requires units of work to be recast as seasons. It is possible to fit some aspects of the sport education season into conventional lessons slots in the timetable, but other features such as cross-curriculum work and festivity are constrained by this arrangement. An activist pedagogical model for working with girls requires a Building the Foundation phase. This involves some classroom-based lessons (though these can be done at a stretch in a gym) and then sampling of a variety of activities chosen by the girls in consultation with their teacher. In practice, this process of opening up the universe of possibilities of what physical education can be, a pedagogy of possibility, runs against the conventional practice of planning by units of work. The teaching personal and social responsibility model requires the very specific tailoring of activities to meet the individual needs of young people that may not be easily contained within a regular timetabled lesson slot. A pedagogical model for outdoor and adventure activities most obviously reaches out beyond the single or double period lesson and the school itself.

We might add to the timetable issues raised by the needs of particular pedagogical models more generic issues that challenge the musical-chairs timetable in secondary schools, and also conventional practice in the primary school. The assumption is made that grouping learners by age is the only way to organise their learning experiences. The notion of Vertically Integrated Projects (VIPS), very popular in some higher education institutions, bring together learners of different ages and stages of education to work on specific projects. The benefits of such an approach have yet to be tested in mainstream practice in primary and secondary schools. Similarly, the notion of blended learning, which involves a mix of face-to-face and technologically-enhanced teaching and learning (see for example, Fernandez-Rio & Bernabe-Martín, 2019; Sargent & Casey, 2020), challenges the assumptions behind the conventional musical-chairs timetable that learning can only take place at specific times and in specific places.

Spaces for teaching and learning: facilities

Space provides a second coordinate to time and is equally as fundamental to the operation and organisation of all educational institutions, even those that work entirely in so-called "virtual space." For physical education, the classroom spaces are most commonly the multi-purpose games hall, fitness gym, playing fields and, if especially well-endowed, a swimming pool, tennis courts and a running track. For the operation of multi-activity, sport technique-based physical education, the timetable works hand-in-hand with the available facilities to place particular age cohorts into specific curriculum activities that are possible to pursue in these facilities. Indeed, they are timetabled with predetermined monikers which are hard to shake (i.e. the "playing fields" or the "games hall"). On the playing fields, major team games of soccer, rugby, field hockey, cricket and rounders. In the games hall, basketball, netball, gymnastics, dance. In the gym, fitness activities. And so on.

It is certainly interesting to speculate who the architects of new school buildings consult before they commit their designs to paper. These conventional spaces may be informed as much (or more) by the architects' own biographies as students than by conversations with physical educators. Once again, Dave Munrow provides as insight into this issue with reference to the 20th century.

> Throughout the early years of the century we sowed the seeds for a gymnastic approach to physical education and we have reaped the harvest of 60 ft by 30 ft gymnasia 'fully equipped.' . . . It is not the local authority's fault that we now find we need weights instead of wall bars [and] canoes instead of window-ladders.
>
> (Munrow, 1963, p. 273)

His point, and ours, is that the spaces made available for learning shape the pedagogies that can be practiced. If a learning space has 100 fixed chairs all facing the same direction, and a raised platform, desk and whiteboard at the front of the room (a classic design for university lecture theatres) then it is difficult to practice anything other than a directive form of teaching and learning, that is, lecturing, (though not impossible). It is also possible to use a grass rugby field for the practice of a cooperative learning pedagogical model, but this may be a somewhat inefficient and expensive use of this facility when other less expensive and easier to maintain facilities would suffice.

We suggest, then, that spaces for learning should be informed by the pedagogical approach to physical education, rather than the nature of the facility (e.g. a 60' by 30' gymnasium) dictating the pedagogy. Nor should pedagogy be informed only by the conventional notions of physical education possessed by architects or educational policy officers of governments.

In proposing MbP, and along with its partner coordinate for the operation and organisation of schools, the timetable, we are suggesting that physical educators need to be making the case for the kinds of facilities and timetable arrangements best suited to this approach. We suggest how they might do this later in this chapter, as members of local collaborative MbP hubs, and wider networks of hubs.

To provide some examples of our own thinking on this issue of spaces for learning, we propose that MbP would be best facilitated through the provision of multi-purpose facilities, with easily adjustable and adaptable fixtures and fittings to suit learners' needs. So, for instance, expensive to provide and maintain playing fields with standard goals and sizes of area are not what is required for the vast majority of students. In contrast to these traditional facilities, multi-use facilities and adaptable equipment are increasingly available to schools. Similarly, indoor areas that are already multi-purpose perhaps need to have adjacent classroom space so that more blended forms of learning are possible. They should not be, as is often the case currently, the spaces where only high stakes examination physical education can be taught.

As for timetabling for MbP, it should be clear that the conventional arrangements of the single or double period in secondary schools impose constraints for many pedagogical models that are less than ideal or that undermine their potential educational benefits entirely. We suggest we need to make the case for the blocks of time, perhaps whole mornings or afternoons, that would allow particular pedagogical models to be implemented more faithfully. Some, such as cooperative learning and teaching personal and social responsibility, may be best done as "short and fat" rather than "long and thin" units of work, where intensive learning experiences are likely to be more effective than regular but brief classes.

Educational purposes: an ID^2 of physical education-as-health promotion

The example offered earlier of the Queensland primary school teachers' purposes behind *when* they timetabled physical education in the school day reveals some commonplace and widespread assumptions about the purposes and value of physical education. Notwithstanding what educational benefits were listed in the Queensland curriculum policy documents of the time, the real purposes of physical education for the teachers are revealed through this malleable act of timetabling. In this case, physical education was considered by some teachers to be of little value in itself, though most teachers did agree that the daily 15 minutes of exercise combatted the emerging curse of obesity. It was instead useful for purging children of their excess energy or, on the other hand, shaking off their lethargy by "blowing away the cobwebs," all the better to improve children's concentration for studying the genuinely educational activities of literacy and numeracy.

In secondary school physical education programs, we can see how the timetable reveals other assumptions about purposes. As we outlined in detail in Chapter 1, the internal order of physical education programs, based on single lessons of around 50 minutes and sometimes double lessons built into short units of work of up to six or eight of these lessons, provides insufficient time for learning. Within the musical-chairs timetable, whole classes of students are on the move around the school every hour or so for much of the day. By the time they depart a classroom-based lesson and reach the physical education department and change into their physical education clothing, 50 minutes becomes 30 minutes of potential learning time at best. In these circumstances, what can teachers do when faced with classes of up to 30 students of varying levels of interest, ability and behaviour? The conscientious teachers teach the techniques of games and sports and occasionally permit students to try to apply them in a game context.

This is how the timetable and associated facilities available to schools produce the real purposes of physical education, regardless of what curriculum policies say. Young people are occupied and active for a majority of the lesson time available. Whether learning is taking place is another matter. Again, as we did in Chapter 1, we stress that teachers have an unenviable task here, and many do the best they can in these completely unsatisfactory circumstances. Nevertheless, the gesture towards skill learning that underpins this pragmatic compromise at the heart of much physical education in both primary and secondary schools is one that takes performance of sports and games as its mostly unarticulated purpose. The ubiquitous assumption is that we offer young people a variety of sports, games and other physical activities in the hope they will find something they enjoy and will engage in a physically active lifestyle (Kirk, 2010).

In order to facilitate the implementation of MbP, we think that a consensus is required on the overarching educational purposes of physical education. It is revealing that many initial teacher education programs in universities require individual student teachers to articulate *their* "philosophy" of physical education, in other words, to be clear about their personal view of educational purposes. While we applaud the intent of colleague teacher educators in this, we think the individualisation of this process is unhelpful. National and more local curriculum policies, which we will discuss next, will state particular preferences for the educational benefits of physical education.

Specific pedagogical models, as we have shown throughout this book, identify distinctive and unique learning aspirations.

We argued in Chapter 1 for a strengths-based concept of physical education's educational purposes, drawing on the work of Quennerstedt, McCuaig and others (see McCuaig, Quennerstedt, & Macdonald, 2013; McCuaig & Quennerstedt, 2018; Quennerstedt, 2008) on the application of a salutogenic notion of health. In this context, we think the over-arching notion that requires consensus amongst teachers, teacher educators, policymakers and perhaps even architects of school buildings, is of physical education-as-health promotion, informed by salutogenesis. This, as Kirk (2010) would put it, is the idea of the idea of physical education, or the ID^2. This would directly challenge the overarching ID^2 of sport technique-based physical education that has dominated throughout the second half of the 20th century and the first decade of this century. Indeed, as Kirk (2020) has argued, there are signs that curriculum policy in the countries of the Global North is increasingly shifting to a view of physical education's overarching educational purposes to be articulated within a health and well-being framework.

Broad and bold curriculum policies and the facilitation of MbP

There have been advocacies for a health-based approach to physical education since at least the 1980s on the coat-tails of what Crawford (1980) called the "new health consciousness" (e.g. Harris, 2005). As we noted in Chapter 1, Sallis and McKenzie's (1991) embrace of the "New Public Health" positioned physical education within the concept of "exercise is medicine," motivated by the pathogenic impulse to reduce the risk of diseases related to sedentariness and, later, obesity. However, throughout the late 20th and early 21st centuries, and much to the chagrin of advocates, this health perspective has remained of marginal interest within the dominant configuration of sport technique-based physical education.

Over the past two decades, however, national curriculum policy development in a growing number of countries has begun to position physical education explicitly within a health framework (Kirk, 2020). Examples include Australia, where in the Australian (national) Curriculum the subject is known as Health and Physical Education (ACARA, 2015); Ontario, Canada, where it is also titled Health and Physical Education; and in Scotland, where physical education sits within the Health and Well-being area of the school curriculum (Education Scotland, 2017). Even where physical education remains the main nomenclature, health forms a significant part of the rationale for its place in the curriculum (e.g. SHAPE America, 2014; Ministry of Education Singapore, 2014).

Only Australia among these examples takes a strengths-based approach informed by salutogenesis, with others tending to be informed by the pathogenic perspective on risk minimisation and prevention, focused on concepts of physical activity and physical fitness. We think a salutogenic approach better serves an ID^2 of physical education-as-health promotion since it is suited to embracing a holistic approach to health and well-being, crucial at a time where pedagogies of affect are required within increasingly prevalent precarity in countries of the Global North (Kirk, 2020).

What is important, however, from the point of view of implementing MbP in physical education, is that school curriculum policies are also what the Organization for Economic Cooperation and Development (OECD) (2015) calls "broad and bold" compared to "specific and less bold." They note a trend towards broad and bold designs such as "guidelines," "models" and "frameworks," with associated "strands" and "learning areas" in many countries around the world (UNESCO & IBE, 2013). Compared with specific and less bold designs, broad and bold curricula, in principle at least, give teachers more control over and responsibility for curriculum-making at local levels, what Priestley, Edwards, Miller, and Priestley (2012, p. 210) call "spaces for manoeuvre." We say "in principle" because in many national education systems, particularly where secondary schooling is dominated by high stakes external exams, teacher agency is seriously circumscribed. This is not the case for physical education in most countries. Even where high stakes exams are well-established, in countries such as Australia, Ireland, New Zealand and the UK, non-examinable "core" physical education remains available to all young people.

As we pointed out in Chapters 1 and 2, when pedagogical models are understood as design specifications for practice, rather than prescribed programs to be implemented to the letter, teacher agency is of crucial importance. And as we noted in Chapter 2, where transformation and change are inevitable and desirable aspects of curriculum implementation, spaces for manoeuvre are required so that teachers can develop programs, based on the guidance provided by national or district curricula, that best meet local needs and interests. Physical educators cannot dictate the terms of overarching national curricula in their home countries and states. But they are usually consulted in some way or another, perhaps through professional association representation in the curriculum writing process, or by survey, in relation to their specific field of interest. Where such opportunities arise, it will be important that curriculum designs are broad and bold so that teachers and other local stakeholders have opportunities to implement MbP.

Teacher professional learning

The importance and desirability of teacher lifelong learning is now well-established in the teacher education literature (MacPhail & Lawson, 2020). The patchwork of random short courses offered by "expert" providers external to the school characterised the continuing professional development of physical education teachers for many years. This approach was roundly criticised by Armour and Yelling (2007) as lacking coherence and more likely to further entrench than challenge multi-activity, sport technique-based physical education.

Appropriately for MbP, which requires the development of local programs, over the past two decades the weight of scholarly opinion has come around to the view that the most effective forms of professional learning in most cases are school-based (Postholm & Wæge, 2016). The location of teacher professional learning in the context in which teachers work has the obvious benefit of strong ecological validity. It is, moreover, a natural extension of the notion of practitioner inquiry which has gained considerable momentum since its emergence in education contexts in the 1980s (Kemmis, McTaggart, & Nixon, 2014). Additional support for school-based teacher professional learning derives from the now widespread view that initial teacher education courses provide only a starting point in the process of preparing teachers for the complexities of work in schools, and that teacher professional learning should be a life-long process (Korthagen, 2005).

Teachers may have experienced one or more pedagogical models in their initial teacher education, or as part of their continuing professional learning. Teachers' experiences of using single pedagogical models is an important building block for MbP. But this experience, while necessary to take forward a program of MbP, is not sufficient in itself. Since, as we argued in Chapters 1 and 2, there are few if any actual examples of MbP in existence, physical education teachers as a professional group lack experience of and expertise in MbP. This suggests the need for comprehensive programs of teacher professional learning to support the roll-out, updating and maintenance of MbP, so that teachers and their collaborators are able to collect evidence of the educational benefits of this approach and to use this evidence to share good practice and inform future decision-making.

We suggest that school-based teacher professional learning has much to offer in terms of improving practice and thus benefitting student learning. But school-based teacher professional learning is also complex and highly variable, as Timperley, Wilson, Barrar, and Fung (2008) have shown, since it is so strongly influenced by the context in which it takes place. Since no two schools are exactly alike, there can be no "silver bullets" for teacher professional learning or, as Leiberman (1995) states, no one-size-fits-all approach. It is possible, nevertheless, to take forward programs of teacher professional learning to support MbP, particularly where these are carried out in collaboration with other stakeholders. Indeed, as Lawson, Kirk, and MacPhail (2020) argue, the professional development challenge for physical education is to bring the education of student teachers, teachers and teacher educators into alignment. They point out several ways in which this might happen. For example, a common feature of teacher education programs is the teacher educators' school visits to support student teachers and their teacher-mentors. This process has the potential to provide powerful means of advancing the professional learning of all three in tandem. This insight also suggests that teachers alone should not shoulder the responsibility for the implementation of MbP in physical education. Instead, and while teachers remain key players, other stakeholders in this process should work in collaboration with teachers.

Locality, stakeholders, hubs and networks

The notion of locality in educational innovation has had a somewhat understated presence for some time in the research literature (see for example Kirk & Macdonald, 2001; Spillane, 1999). When it is mentioned, it is most often associated with practitioner researchers working within communities of practice (Enthoven & de Bruijn, 2010) and innovation supported by local collaboration (Gustavsen, Nyhan, & Ennals, 2007). We think this notion of locality is crucial to the successful implementation of MbP in physical education, for several reasons.

The first of these is acknowledgement of the importance of the development of local school programs. Pedagogical models, as we have characterised them in this book, are premised on recognition that the translation and transformation of innovative ideas through the process of implementation is inevitable and desirable. Pedagogical models seek to manage the tension between sources of innovation external to schools and the agency of teachers and other local stakeholders. So, for example, even though two schools may implement a physical education program based on sport education, maintaining strong fidelity to the practice architectures and the main idea, critical elements and learning aspirations, we would expect the local program in each school to look different, at least to some degree.

A second reason for the importance of locality is that expertise resides in local contexts of implementation that do not exist elsewhere. Teachers, students and parents are better placed to know what local needs and interest may be, and what challenges for physical education exist in localities, than agents who work external to the school. The folly of ignoring or even attempting to eliminate this expertise through so-called "teacher-proofing" educational innovation has been well demonstrated through the years.

A third reason is that relationships are sustainable because face-to-face contact over time is possible. Locality facilitates regular contact and collaboration because, in practical terms, distances to travel for face-to-face contact are feasible and relatively inexpensive. More than this, people who share a locality are likely to share aspects of the culture of the places that constitute and construct that locality. They are also likely to have interests in common.

The stakeholders in a locality will vary from place to place. In addition to the student teacher, teacher, teacher educator triumvirate already mentioned, we can add students and school leaders. Parents also have a stake in their child's physical education experiences, though the extent to which this is expressed in active participation of some kind, for example as volunteers, will vary. In addition to teacher educators, who may be mostly university-based, researchers will also be important stakeholders. Sometimes teacher educators and researchers may be the same person, and sometimes not. Local Authority officers, where they exist, will be important stakeholders and possibly gatekeepers for access by individuals and organisations external to schools. In some cases, community sports clubs and other organisations that provide access to physical activity may be stakeholders.

We propose that stakeholders together form research and development hubs to take forward the implementation of MbP. These hubs can be thought of, in turn, as networked learning communities. In physical education there has been a number of recent studies that have built on the related concept of communities of practice, informed by the foundational work on situated learning by Lave and Wenger (1991), (e.g. MacPhail, Patton, Parker, & Tannehill, 2014; Rhoades & Woods, 2013). These studies have found consistently that collaboration empowers teachers, provides emotional support, and enriches and enhances teacher learning. They might also be a powerful means by which local stakeholders are consulted on important issues influencing the practice of physical education, from the development of state or national curricula to the design of new school buildings.

According to Day and Townsend (2009), networked learning communities are based on four principles: voluntarism, choice, agency and ownership. Participation must be voluntary on the part of all participants. There can be no mandated "requirement" for membership of a MbP hub. Agency is a feature of the participation of all members of the community, though as Kirk and Macdonald (2001) explain, with each agreeing their specific remit based on their positionality with the local context. Choice thus is a key principle, with all participants having a say in the priorities a MbP hub identifies and how its members pursue these. Finally, the work of the hub is owned by its members. For there to be genuine buy-in by all stakeholders, the stakes must be determined by and matter to them collectively as well as individually.

Notwithstanding the paramount importance we give to locality and collaborative hubs for the successful implementation of MbP in physical education, we recognise that hubs will require input and support from other, not so local, places. We have already discussed the importance of district and national curricula that are broad and bold enough to accommodate MbP. Moreover, we think it is asking too much of localities, in particular teachers, students and school leaders, to be the sole generators of innovative ideas for MbP. The participation of external agents to the school such as teacher educators, researchers and Local Authority officers offers one avenue for support for regular evaluation and refreshment of ideas and practices locally. One possibility specific to MbP may be that local hubs link up to form wider networks within regions. These networks could be a medium for sharing good practice beyond localities. They could, in turn, offer input to other organisations that have a wider geographical remit, such as national professional organisations for teachers for instance, in the UK, the Association for Physical Education and the Scottish Association of Teachers of Physical Education, and research organisations for example, the Scottish and British Educational Research Associations.

Conclusion

Our purpose in this chapter was to identify and discuss some of the conditions that are required to be met in order to implement and sustain MbP in physical education in schools and related pedagogical sites. We considered time and the timetable, spaces for teaching and learning, educational purposes and the ID^2 of physical education, curriculum frameworks, teacher professional learning, and the central place of locality in this scheme and associated notions of collaborative hubs and networks. For some of these conditions to be met, such as a different approach to timetabling, particularly in secondary schools, and appropriate forms of national or state-wide curricula, actions are required that go beyond the remit of any individual teacher or researcher, or the organisations to which they may be belong. Conditions such as these require careful communications and negotiations and perhaps the creation of new structures to take them forward. Other conditions, while similarly challenging, nevertheless are already available to us or are within our collective power to create them.

Consequently, while the pursuit of MbP in physical education may seem to require radical reform, at least to some degree, we hope that this chapter shows we already have some of the means to satisfying many of these conditions. We offer this discussion as the beginnings of a route map towards a MbP future for physical education, which we expect to be redrafted and strengthened over time as it is tested by practice.

Perhaps the greatest challenge and most radical aspect of this proposal is that for these conditions to be met, levels of collaboration, communication, and consensus that have all too frequently in the past been absent within the physical education community, will be required. Our rationale for MbP, built in Chapters 1 and 2, attempts to make a persuasive case that whatever actions we take over the future forms of our field, we cannot continue to trust that the status quo of the currently dominant multi-activity, sport technique-based programs is sustainable and educationally appropriate. We argued in these chapters that physical education has much more to offer young people than this dominant approach can deliver. At the same time, the considerable sums of public money that are spent to support this failing form of the subject cannot be guaranteed to continue unless we can provide evidence of genuine educational benefits to all young people of their engagement in school physical education.

This is a challenge we will sooner or later have to address. We need everyone who holds a stake in physical education to step forward and take up this challenge.

References

Armour, K. A., & Yelling, M. (2007). Effective professional development for physical education teachers: The role of informal, collaborative learning. *Journal of Teaching in Physical Education, 26*, 177–200.

Australian Curriculum, Assessment and Reporting Authority (ACARA). (2015). *Australian curriculum health and physical education.* Retrieved from www.australiancurriculum.edu.au/f-10-curriculum/health-and-physical-education/rationale/

Chanan, G., & Gilchrist, L. (1974). *What school is for.* London: Methuen.

Crawford, R. (1980). Healthism and the medicalization of everyday life. *International Journal of Health Services, 10*(3), 365–388.

Day, C., & Townsend, A. (2009). Practitioner action research: Building and sustaining success through networked learning communities. In B. Somekh & S. E. Noffke (Eds.), *The Sage handbook of educational action research* (pp. 178–189). London: Sage.

Education Scotland. (2017). *Curriculum for excellence, benchmarks for physical education.* Retrieved from https://education.gov.scot/improvement/Documents/HWBPhysicalEducationBenchmarksPDF.pdf

Enthoven, M., & de Bruijn, E. (2010). Beyond locality: The creation of public practice-based knowledge through practitioner research in professional learning communities and communities of practice. A review of three books on practitioner
research and professional communities. *Educational Action Research*, *18*(2),
289–298.

Fernandez-Rio, J., & Bernabe-Martín, J. (2019). Facebook and sport education:
Mirroring the model at home to promote parental involvement. *Sport, Education
and Society*, *24*(8), 814–827.

Gatto, J. T. (1993). *Dumbing us down: The hidden curriculum of compulsory schooling*. Gabriola Island, BC: New Society Publishers.

Gustavsen, B., Nyhan, B., & Ennals, R. (2007). *Learning together for local innovation: Promoting learning regions*. Luxemburg: CEDEFOP.

Harris, J. (2005). Health-related exercise and physical education. In K. Green & K.
Hardman (Eds.), *Physical education: Essential issues* (pp. 78–97). London: Sage.

Kemmis, S., McTaggart, R., & Nixon, R. (2014). *Critical participatory action
research*. Singapore: Springer.

Kirk, D. (2010). *Physical education futures*. London: Routledge.

Kirk, D. (2020). *Precarity, critical pedagogy and physical education*. London:
Falmer.

Kirk, D., & Macdonald, D. (2001). Teacher voice and ownership of curriculum
change. *Journal of Curriculum Studies*, *33*(5), 551–567.

Korthagen, F. (2005). Practice, theory and person in life-long professional lean-
ing. In D. Beijaard, P. C. Meijer, G. Morine-Dershimer, & H. Tillema (Eds.),
Teacher professional development in changing conditions (pp. 79–94). New
York: Springer.

Lave, J., & Wenger, E. (1991). *Situated learning: Legitimate peripheral participation in communities of practice*. New York: Cambridge University Press.

Lawson, H. A., Kirk, D., & MacPhail, A. (2020). The professional development challenge: Achieving desirable outcomes for students, teachers and teacher educators.
In A. MacPhail & H. A. Lawson (Eds.), *School physical education and teacher
education: Collaborative redesign for the twenty-first century* (pp. 141–152).
London: Routledge.

Leiberman, A. (1995). Practices that support teacher development: Transforming
conceptions of professional learning. *Phi Delta Kappa*, *76*(8), 591–596.

MacPhail, A., & Lawson, H. A. (2020). *School physical education and teacher education: Collaborative redesign for the twenty-first century*. London: Routledge.

MacPhail, A., Patton, K., Parker, M., & Tannehill, D. (2014). Leading by example:
Teacher educators' professional learning through communities of practice. *Quest*,
66, 39–56.

McCuaig, L., & Quennerstedt, M. (2018). Health by stealth – exploring the sociocultural dimensions of salutogenesis for sport, health and physical education
research. *Sport, Education and Society*, *23*(2), 111–122.

McCuaig, L., Quennerstedt, M., & Macdonald, D. (2013). A salutogenic, strengths-
based approach as a theory to guide HPE curriculum change. *Asia-Pacific Journal
of Health, Sport and Physical Education*, *4*(2), 109–125.

Ministry of Education Singapore. (2014). *Physical education teaching and learning syllabus*. Retrieved from www.moe.gov.sg/docs/default-source/document/ education/syllabuses/physical-sports-education/files/physical_education_sylla bus_2014.pdf

Munrow, A. D. (1963). *Pure and applied gymnastics* (2nd ed.). London: Bell.

Organization for Economic Cooperation and Development (OECD). (2015). *Improving schools in Scotland: An OECD perspective*. Paris: OECD.

Postholm, M. B., & Wæge, K. (2016). Teachers' learning in school-based development. *Educational Research, 58*, 24–38.

Priestley, M., Edwards, R., Miller, K., & Priestley, A. (2012). Teacher agency in curriculum-making: Agents of change and spaces for manoeuvre. *Curriculum Inquiry, 42*(2), 191–214.

Quennerstedt, M. (2008). Exploring the relation between physical activity and health – a salutogenic approach to physical education. *Sport, Education and Society, 13*(3), 267–283.

Rhoades, J. L., & Woods, A. (2013). Self-organized communities of practice in physical education. *Quest, 65*, 44–56.

Sallis, J. F., & McKenzie, T. L. (1991). Physical education's role in public health. *Research Quarterly for Exercise and Sport, 62*(2), 124–137.

Sargent, J., & Casey, A. (2020). Flipped learning, pedagogy and digital technology: Establishing consistent practice to optimise lesson time. *European Physical Education Review, 26*(1), 70–84.

SHAPE America. (2014). *Grade-level outcomes for k-12 physical education*. Retrieved from www.shapeamerica.org/standards/pe/upload/Grade-Level-Out comes-for-K-12-Physical-Education.pdf

Spillane, J. P. (1999). External reform initiatives and teachers' efforts to reconstruct their practice: The mediating role of teachers' zones of enactment. *Journal of Curriculum Studies, 31*(2), 143–175.

Timperley, H., Wilson, A., Barrar, H., & Fung, I. (2008). *Teacher professional learning and development: Best evidence synthesis iteration*. Wellington: Ministry of Education.

Tinning, R. I., & Kirk, D. (1991). *Daily physical education: Collected papers on health based physical education in Australia*. Geelong: Deakin University Press.

UNESCO & IBE. (2013). *Glossary of curriculum terminology*. Geneva: UNESCO.

Index

Note: Page numbers in *italic* indicate a figure and page numbers in **bold** indicate a table on the corresponding page.